THE SPIRITUALITY OF MARTYRDOM ... TO THE LIMITS OF LOVE

Servais Pinckaers, OP

THE SPIRITUALITY OF MARTYRDOM . . . TO THE LIMITS OF LOVE

Translated by
Patrick M. Clark & Annie Hounsokou

The Catholic University of America Press
Washington, D.C.

Original French edition: *La spiritualité du martyre . . . jusqu'au bout de l'Amour*

The paper used in this publication meets the minimum requirements of American National Standards for Information Science—Permanence of Paper for Printed Library Materials, ANSI Z39.48-1984.

∞

Cataloging-in-Publication Data available from
the Library of Congress

ISBN: 978-0-8132-2853-2

CONTENTS

TRANSLATOR'S PREFACE

THEOLOGICAL CONTEXT AND GENRE OF THE PRESENT STUDY

Fr. Servais Pinckaers, OP, perhaps more than any other scholar, has contributed to the renewal of Catholic moral theology since the Second Vatican Council. *The Sources of Christian Ethics*, which many consider to be Pinckaers's magnum opus, has found an extraordinarily wide readership in the English-speaking world.[1] It is an introduction to the field as sweeping as it is compelling, beginning with a constructive account of the fundamental nature and aims of Christian ethics as an academic discipline: "Christian ethics," he writes "is the branch of theology that studies human acts so as to direct them to a loving vision of God seen as our true, complete happiness and our final end."[2] By establishing from the outset theology's primary concern with God, his work has breathed fresh life into the field of moral theology by simply echoing the tradi-

1. Servais Pinckaers, OP, *Sources de la moral chrétienne* (Fribourg: University Press Fribourg, 1985); translated into English by Sr. Mary Thomas Noble as *Sources of Christian Ethics* (Washington, D.C.: The Catholic University of America Press, 1995). I will refer to this work simply as *Sources* from this point.

2. Ibid., 8. The definition also includes this qualifying sentence, immediately following: "This vision is attained by means of grace, the virtues, and the gifts, in the light of revelation and reason."

tional Christian claim that human action is ultimately ordered to participation in divine life. All of the most salient and influential arguments of Pinckaers's thought appear in *Sources*: the reprioritization of scripture in moral theology, the reestablishment of happiness as a central category for Christian ethics, and the proper differentiation of the rival concepts of freedom in the contemporary Christian imagination. These have proven to be powerful and exciting ideas and have reenergized many minds and classrooms dedicated to the study of Catholic moral theology.

Yet there are hidden gems in the *Sources* as well, passages that open up to us some of the determinative fault lines in Pinckaers's thought. One such passage appears rather early on in the text, in the chapter dealing with the Sermon on the Mount.[3] The immediate context of this particular passage is Pinckaers's attempt to reestablish the sermon's importance for Christian ethics.[4] For him, the Sermon on the Mount represents nothing less than the definitive scriptural elaboration of the New Law.[5] In the course of his ensuing exposition of Augustine's commentary on the Beatitudes and his correlation of them with the seven gifts of the Holy Spirit and the seven petitions of the *Our Father*, Pinckaers also inserts a brief aside explaining Augustine's interpretation of the eighth Beatitude, "blessed are those who are persecuted for righteousness'

3. Pinckaers, chap. 6, "The Sermon on the Mount and Christian Ethics," in *Sources*.

4. Pinckaers bases this claim principally on Augustine's characterization of the Sermon as the "perfect model of the Christian life" in Augustine, *Commentary on the Sermon on the Mount* 1.1, as translated by Jarosłav Pelikan in *The Preaching of St. Augustine: "Our Lord's Sermon on the Mount"* (Philadelphia: Fortress Press, 1973), 1.

5. Aquinas defines the New Law as "the presence of the Holy Spirit in the souls of the faithful" (*Summa Theologiae* I-II, q. 108, a. 1). Aquinas gleans this definition from Augustine's treatise *De spiritu et littera* 36 (XXI); see *Catechism of the Catholic Church*, 2nd ed. (Washington, D.C.: United States Catholic Conference, 2000) [1965–75]. This and all subsequent quotations from the *Summa Theologiae* (*ST*) are from the translation of the Fathers of the English Dominican Province (New York: Benziger Bros., 1947).

sake, for theirs is the kingdom of heaven" (Mt 5:10). For Augustine, he writes, "the eighth Beatitude included and confirmed all the others. It represented humanity in all its perfection.... This is the final achievement of the work undertaken and brought to completion by the Holy Spirit."[6] Though Pinckaers does not pursue the point further in *Sources*, it does offer the reader a brief glimpse into Pinckaers's understanding of the perfection of the Christian life. At the very least, it suggests the high degree of significance that Pinckaers attaches to Christian martyrdom.

The present book helps to flesh out this significance, both within the broader scope of the Christian theological tradition and within the more limited scope of his own moral thought. However, the book should not be viewed as a broad survey of the history of Christian martyrdom, nor does it aspire to offer a systematic theological account. Inspired as it is by Pinckaers's university teaching and influenced as it is by his predominant expertise in Catholic moral theology, the present book approaches the topic of Christian martyrdom from a particular angle that not every reader may find ultimately satisfying. As indicated by the title, Fr. Pinckaers's principal aim is to give a theological account of the *spirituality* of Christian martyrdom, a spirituality that in turn provides the moral paradigm in which the act of martyrdom may intelligibly be regarded as, in St. Thomas's words, "the greatest proof of the perfection of charity."[7]

What Pinckaers seeks to demonstrate in this selective study is not so much the instrumental role martyrdom played in the

6. *Sources*, 154. Here is the pertinent passage from Augustine's *Commentary* (4.12): "This eighth maxim, which returns to the beginning and declares the perfect man, is perhaps also signified by the circumcision on the eighth day in the Old Testament, by the resurrection of the Lord after the Sabbath, which is surely the eighth and at the same time the first day, and by the celebration of the octave of the feast which we observe on the occasion of the regeneration of the new man, and by the number itself of Pentecost"; Pelikan, *Preaching of St. Augustine*, 12.

7. *ST* II-II, q. 124, a. 3.

church's "fertility" in the ancient world, but rather the central normative role it played in the moral imagination of the Christian community. Pinckaers focuses on those places within the apostolic and patristic periods that he takes to be most pivotal in the development and dissemination of this paradigm and then attempts to point out how that paradigm has gone on to influence the vital sources of modern Catholic moral thought and life. These sources include not only pivotal theological figures such as Ignatius of Antioch, Augustine, and Aquinas, but more general bodies of doctrine as well, especially those pertaining to the Eucharist and eschatology.

This book is therefore a classic exercise in *ressourcement*, a "return to the sources" so as to reorient and refresh the present theological task. The larger theological task in Pinckaers's case is the renewal of Catholic moral theology in the wake of the early modern "manualist tradition," which largely viewed the Christian life as the fulfillment of various obligations rather than a graced growth in the virtues. When viewed against this larger project, the rationale and value of this book become most clear. For obligation-based models of ethics, martyrdom is inevitably portrayed as "supererogatory" or viewed as "a counsel for the perfect" rather than a natural outgrowth (however rare) of the theological virtues to which every Christian is called. Not only does the book fill an important gap in Pinckaers's moral thought, but it also provides a brief outline of the theological paradigm of Christian martyrdom that can stand on its own, either within an instructional setting or for personal enrichment. As one progresses through the book, one can easily envision oneself in the classroom of this master teacher, and God willing, those who are familiar with Pinckaers will be able to hear his distinctive voice in these lessons with which he clearly took so much care.

REMARKS ON THE TRANSLATION

Though the merit of Pinckaers's scholarship stands on its own, his writing style nonetheless adds a certain beauty and nuance to his work, which as translators Annie Hounsokou and I, have attempted to preserve in this little book. Thus we have tried to render his French as literally as possible without losing his distinctive voice along the way. As with any translation, idioms and grammatical discrepancies forced us to take some small liberties in order to maintain the style and flow of the text. The fact that the book was adapted from lecture notes also sometimes presented the challenge of turning partially formulated phrases or fragments into complete sentences that not only conformed to English grammar but also fit within his larger progression of thought. That being said, we have made little effort to anglicize the text in any uniform way, and so many readers may hear the French original coming through in places. We do not regard these Gallic overtones of the text to be an obstacle to its clarity, however. Indeed, we even hope they might serve as another way in which the translation may bring the reader into more immediate contact with this important and saintly figure of twentieth-century Catholic theology.

The subtitle of this book serves as a good example of the sorts of difficulties faced by translators. The original French, "*jusqu'au bout de l'Amour*," is a lyricism whose various possible translations all seem to suggest different confused readings in English. The translation of *bout* as "end" preserves the ambiguity of the original, allowing it to mean both "limit" and "culmination," but its connotation of cessation seems stronger in English than in French. Certainly the death of the martyr is a kind of cessation, but the larger premise of the study is that martyrdom displays the perfection of a reality that *never* ends: the divine love that is the end (as in *telos*) of the Christian life.

In addition to these sorts of decisions, there were other more basic decisions we had to make in the process of translation. For the copious biblical passages, for instance, we substituted the *New Revised Standard Version* for Pinckaers's renderings, indicating any necessary deviations with brackets. For quotations from early Christian sources, we provided in almost every instance a standard public domain translation from patristic scholars that we then cited in footnotes. Occasionally we deemed it necessary to include a translator's note on particular passages, either to clarify meaning, indicate stylistic convention, or explain a certain departure from the original French.

RELATION AND CONTRIBUTION TO MARTYRDOM IN THE CONTEMPORARY WORLD

Since the original version of this book was published in 2000, a great many scholarly works on martyrdom in general and Christian martyrdom in particular have appeared. Much of this interest in martyrdom was sparked by the suicide attacks of September 11, 2001, and the appeal to martyrdom made by many of those advocating or employing similar sorts of attacks.[8] There has also been a budding interest in the development of martyrdom as a moral category in Catholic theology, particularly in the wake of the canonizations of Ss. Maximilian Kolbe and Edith Stein by Pope St. John Paul II and the beatification of Bl. Franz Jägerstätter by Pope Benedict XVI. These figures were all declared martyrs, even

8. The work of Brian Wicker is a good example of this sort of approach; see his "Conflict and Martyrdom after 11 September 2001," in *Theology* 106 (May–June 2003): 159–67; "The Drama of Martyrdom: Christian and Muslim Approaches," in *Witnesses to Faith? Martyrdom in Christianity and Islam* (Burlington, Vt.: Ashgate, 2006), 105–16; and Wicker, Peter Bishop, and Maha Azzam, "Martyrdom and Murder: Aspects of Suicidal Terrorism," in *Witnesses to Faith?*, 123–38.

though their deaths did not strictly conform to the traditional criteria of being precipitated by fidelity in the face of manifest "hatred of the faith" (*odium fidei*).[9] These two saints also recall the great quantity and peculiar character of the many thousands of Christians who died in the twentieth century bearing witness to their faith amid conditions of political oppression and injustice.[10] Such violence continues to the present day and by many counts has significantly increased in recent years.[11] All these developments have contributed to a growing body of theological scholarship on martyrdom and even sparked an ongoing debate about the degree to which the significance of martyrdom has been historically exaggerated by Christians and how even now martyrdom discourse may continue to perform certain rhetorical and political functions within communities.[12]

Yet the contemporary theological scholarship on Christian martyrdom goes well beyond what might be occasioned by any set of historical and political developments. Much of this scholarship

9. For an excellent examination of these cases, see Lawrence Cunningham's "Saints and Martyrs: Some Contemporary Considerations," in *Theological Studies* 60, no. 3 (September 1999): 529–38, as well as his "Causa non Poena," in *More Than a Memory* (Dudley, Mass.: Peeters, 2005), 451–64.

10. For a good overview, see Robert Royal's *Catholic Martyrs of the Twentieth Century* (New York: Crossroad, 2000), and Susan Bergman, ed., *Martyrs: Contemporary Writers on Modern Lives of Faith* (Maryknoll, N.Y.: Orbis, 1996); see also Jon Sobrino's novel theological construal of corporate martyrdom in his *Witnesses to the Kingdom: The Martyrs of El Salvador and the Crucified Peoples* (Maryknoll, N.Y.: Orbis, 2003).

11. John L. Allen Jr., *The Global War on Christians: Dispatches from the Front Lines of Anti-Christian Persecution* (New York: Image, 2013).

12. For a taste of this debate, see Candida R. Moss's *The Myth of Persecution* (New York: HarperOne, 2013), and Ephraim Radner's "Unmythical Martyrs," in *First Things: A Monthly Journal of Religion and Public Life*, no. 233 (May 2013): 53–55; see also Elizabeth Castelli, "Religion as a Chain of Memory: Cassie Bernall of Columbine High and the American Legacy of Early Christian Martyrdom," in *Martyrdom and Memory: Gender, Theory and Religion* (New York: Columbia University Press, 2004), 172–96.

is systematic in nature, focusing in particular on the unique correspondence between the martyr's death and the death of Christ himself. Karl Rahner's essay "On Martyrdom" is a paradigmatic example of this speculative approach. According to Rahner, Christians not only believe that death has been overcome by Christ, but maintain that this victory comes precisely in and through death. Thus for him, Christians enter into the fullness of salvation only by "dying the death of Christ, for only Christ's death gained this grace for us and only his death freed our death into the life of God himself."[13] While each and every person may inwardly conform his death to that of Christ's, it is the martyr's death alone that can provide clear external witness to this interior conformity. Hence Rahner concludes that

> a martyr's death is not only death through man's freedom, but also the revelation of death in faith. Martyrdom is, therefore, Christian death as such. It is not only what Christian death in general should be, but it appears as such as well. Martyrdom discloses the essence of Christian death, death in freedom and faith, which otherwise is hidden under the ambiguity of all human events.[14]

The basic notion is that Christians accept suffering and persecution not simply in order to disseminate their message and consolidate their communal identity, but rather because it is what their adherence to Christ demands of them amid the contingencies of a fallen world.[15] Other accounts of the internal motivations of mar-

13. Karl Rahner, *On the Theology of Death* (New York: Herder and Herder, 1964), 88.

14. Ibid., 102.

15. See also Craig Hovey's *To Share in the Body: A Theology of Martyrdom for Today's Church* (Grand Rapids, Mich.: Brazos Press, 2008). Hovey argues there that Christians should never regard the death of martyrs as part of some "evangelistic strategy," to be used instrumentally toward some further end, for to do so would render the Gospel dependent upon the violence of worldly power. In maintaining the intrinsic value of bearing witness to the faith, he writes, "Christians are released from the thought that persecution is necessary for the Church's witness" (37).

tyrs, both secular and theological, have subsequently attempted to account for the various psychological aspects at work in martyrdom.[16] These, however, are not immediately related to the focus of the present book.

More pertinent to the sort of study Pinckaers undertakes here are the numerous historical and patristic studies on martyrdom that have been published in the past two decades. From G.W. Bowersock's landmark 1995 work *Martyrdom and Rome* to Robin Darling Young's seminal 2001 volume entitled *In Procession before the World: Martyrdom as Public Liturgy in Early Christianity*, the writings of many leading patristic scholars have been dedicated to retrieving and critically analyzing the martyrological discourse of early Christianity, with an eye toward a renewed understanding of the role played by martyrdom in the Christian theological tradition more generally.[17] Special mention should be made in this

16. The collection of essays in Margaret Cormack's *Sacrificing the Self* (New York: Oxford University Press, 2002), is a good example of the secular approach to the psychology of the martyr; see also Rona M. Fields's "The Psychology and Sociology of Martyrdom," in *Martyrdom: The Psychology, Theology and Politics of Self-Sacrifice*, edited by Rona M. Fields, Valérie Rosoux, Cóilín Owens, and Michael Berenbaum, 23–82 (Westport, Conn.: Praeger, 2004). For more theological accounts of what motivates the martyr, see Craig Steven Titus's *Resilience and the Virtue of Fortitude: Aquinas in Dialogue with the Psychological Sciences* (Washington, D.C.: The Catholic University of America Press, 2006); Lee H. Yearley's "The Nature-Grace Question in the Context of Fortitude," in *Thomist* 35 (October 1971): 557–80; and J. Warren Smith's "Martyrdom: Self-Denial or Self-Exaltation? Motives for Self-Sacrifice from Homer to Polycarp; A Theological Reflection," in *Modern Theology* 22, no. 2 (April 2006): 169–95. Michael P. Jensen's book *Martyrdom and Identity: The Self on Trial* (New York: T. and T. Clark, 2010), also provides a theologically informed account of the psychology of martyrdom, dealing specifically with the role played by the "self" in Christian martyrological literature.

17. G. W. Bowersock, *Martyrdom and Rome* (New York: Cambridge University Press, 1995); Robin Darling Young, *In Procession before the World: Martyrdom as Public Liturgy in Early Christianity* (Milwaukee, Wisc.: Marquette University Press, 2001); see also Paul Middleton's *Radical Martyrdom and Cosmic Conflict in Early Christianity* (New York: T. and T. Clark, 2006), and Shelly Matthews's

regard to Candida Moss's extensive research in the field of ancient Christian martyrdom. In addition to her magisterial organization and exposition of the major martyrological texts, Moss's interpretive argument that early Christians generally conceived of martyrdom in terms of imitating Jesus is one whose theological implications have yet to be fully explored.[18] Though Pinckaers's own exposition of many of these same texts is nowhere nearly as extensive or exhaustive, his own interpretation of their theological and ethical significance in many ways anticipates Moss's focus upon the central role of imitating Jesus.[19]

The "spirituality of martyrdom," as Pinckaers puts it, permeated the early church not on account of the extraordinary heroism of the martyrs themselves, but first and foremost because Christians saw in martyrdom the pattern by which Christ's own death has transformed the world.[20] For Pinckaers, martyrdom represents the culmination of the Beatitudes, which serve as a sort of

---

Perfect Martyr: The Stoning of Stephen and the Construction of Christian Identity (New York: Oxford University Press, 2010).

18. Candida R. Moss's principal studies thus far are *The Other Christs: Imitating Jesus in Ancient Christian Ideologies of Martyrdom* (New York: Oxford University Press, 2010); *Ancient Christian Martyrdom: Diverse Practices, Theologies and Traditions* (New Haven: Yale University Press, 2012); and *Myth of Persecution*.

19. For other studies of early Christian martyrdom that take up this view, see Brian E. Beck's "'Imitatio Christi' and the Lucan Passion Narrative," in *Suffering and Martyrdom in the New Testament*, edited by William Horbury and Brian McNeil, 28–47 (New York: Cambridge University Press, 2009); Stephen E. Fowl's "Believing Forms Seeing: Formation for Martyrdom in Philippians," in *Character and Scripture: Moral Formation, Community and Biblical Interpretation*, edited by William P. Brown, 317–30 (Grand Rapids, Mich.: William B. Eerdmans, 2002); Isabelle Kinnard's "*Imitatio Christi* in Christian Martyrdom and Asceticism: A Critical Dialogue," in *Asceticism and Its Critics: Historical Accounts and Comparative Perspectives*, edited by Oliver Freiberger, 131–50 (New York: Oxford University Press, 2006); and Robert Louis Wilken's "The Lives of the Saints and the Pursuit of Virtue," in *First Things* 8 (December 1990): 45–51.

20. Pinckaers himself cites these passages as evidence for this claim: Mt 10; Lk 22:31; 1 Pt 1:6–7, 4:12–14.

self-portrait of Christ himself.[21] It is this conformity to Christ, as portrayed in the Beatitudes, that distinguishes the courage of the martyr from that of other ancient heroes. As Pinckaers puts it,

> even while publicly scorned and neglected in prison, [the martyrs] suffered as members of the Body of Christ, in communion with the Church. And so their testimony is still able to resound today in the liturgy of the Church: an appeal to all and an illustration of the greatest of the beatitudes: "Blessed are you ... when they persecute you ... on account of me. Rejoice and be glad!"[22]

Pinckaers is careful to point out that this ecclesial dimension of martyrdom is based not upon the designation of the martyrs as ethical exemplars, as if it were their self-sacrifice on behalf of the community that made them worthy of commemoration and emulation. Rather, it is their association with and embodiment of the Passion of Christ that accounts for the power of the martyr's witness. While the significance of martyrdom in the early church is often summed up with Tertullian's famous adage "the blood of martyrs is the seed of Christians," this simple idea of "persecution leading to proliferation" runs the great risk of omitting the most crucial component of martyrdom for early Christians: personal association with Christ's Passion.[23] As Pinckaers goes on to argue,

> the idea of the fecundity of the blood of martyrs is clearly inspired by the Lord's words as reported by St. John: "If the grain of wheat does not fall to the ground and die, it alone remains; but if it dies, it bears much fruit"

21. *Sources*, 135, 154. For more on Pinckaers's characterization of martyrdom as the culmination of the Beatitudes, see Patrick M. Clark, "Servais Pinckaers's Retrieval of Martyrdom as the Culmination of the Christian Life," *Josephinum Journal of Theology* 17, no. 2 (Summer/Fall 2010): 250–76.

22. Pinckaers, *La spiritualité du martyre ... jusqu'au bout de l'amour* (Paris: Saint-Paul éditions religieuses, 2000), 12.

23. Tertullian, "Apology," ch. 50, in *Ante-Nicene Fathers*, trans. Sydney Thelwall, edited by Alexander Roberts, James Donaldson, and A. Cleveland Coxe (Buffalo, N.Y.: Christian Literature Publishing, 1885), 3:55.

(Jn 12:24). It links the martyrdom of Christians to the Passion of Christ in which this saying of Jesus is first realized, after which it comes to fruition in the members of his mystical Body who are submitted to a similar condemnation and agony. The martyrdom of Christians perpetuates the Passion [in its own mode] just as much as the Eucharist does sacramentally. Therein lies the power of its influence.[24]

Martyrdom was hence regarded by the early church to be a suitable substitute for the sacrament of baptism, effectively incorporating the disciple into the Body of Christ. It was also considered to be a kind of "public Eucharist," in which Christ's real presence was manifested to the world in the body of the martyr. Martyrdom therefore had no less of an ethical orientation for the early Church than the sacraments themselves; and just like the sacraments, the formative power of martyrdom was its capacity to allow one to participate in the person and work of Christ.[25]

Even though the present work does not aspire to a comprehensive treatment of martyrdom within the Christian theological tradition, its focus on the "spirituality of martyrdom" offers a unique contribution to the growing body of contemporary martyrdom scholarship. Beyond the various disputes about the number, motivation, and meaning behind historical instances of violence against Christians, this work seeks to uncover the underlying theological intelligibility of seeing these instances of violence as acts of witness, testifying to the redemptive love communicated

24. Pinckaers, *Spiritualité du Martyre*, 11.

25. This doctrine, traditionally referred to as the "baptism of blood," has been held by the church from at least the patristic age. The *Catechism of the Catholic Church* states that "the Church has always held the firm conviction that those who suffer death for the sake of the faith without having received Baptism are baptized by their death for and with Christ. This *Baptism of blood*, like the *desire for Baptism*, brings about the fruits of Baptism without being a sacrament" (no. 1258). In a similar way, martyrdom was also considered to be a kind of "public Eucharist," in which Christ's real presence was manifested before all. On this point, see Young's 2001 Père Marquette Lectures, published in *In Procession before the World*.

to the world through the cross of Jesus Christ. Pinckaers aims to give an account of how this way of viewing such acts—namely, as a participation in Christ's own self-sacrificial death—emerges and develops within the Catholic theological tradition. At the very least, his main thesis is a salutary reminder of a fundamental but often forgotten premise of the Christian understanding of martyrdom—namely, that it is not something that is apprehended only through prior theological categories, but rather serves as the lens through which all other theological categories are viewed. Pinckaers reminds us that martyrdom is thus the primordial paradigm of Christian spirituality through which all other subsequent modes emerge. Such a thesis is no less significant for being unoriginal! Indeed, *ressourcement* theology is at its best when it limits itself to this kind of anamnetic task, a task that Fr. Pinckaers performs here with his characteristic *pathos* and *élan*.

Patrick M. Clark

THE SPIRITUALITY OF MARTYRDOM ...TO THE LIMITS OF LOVE

FOREWORD

No one, it seems, spontaneously desires to suffer martyrdom. No one wants to die amid torture and insults, or even simply to experience physical pain. Yet countless Christians, from the first generations in Palestine, Greece, and Rome, willingly accepted martyrdom and went to their deaths with a confidence and joy reminiscent of the final Beatitude:[1] "Blessed are those who are persecuted for righteousness' sake.... Rejoice and be glad, for your reward is great in heaven" (Mt 5:10, 12).[2] They became paradigms of Christian discipleship, passing on to others a desire for martyrdom that one continues to find [even] in modern saints such as St. Dominic and St. Teresa of Avila. The stories of the acts of the martyrs were to become the first books of spirituality alongside the scriptures, the first such being the Acts of the Apostles, which de-

1. We have chosen to capitalize the word "beatitude" when it is used to refer to one of the eight phrases at the beginning of Matthew 5, which normally go under the title "the Beatitudes," in order to distinguish that particular usage of the term from its other principal usage in this text, which refers to the more general notion of happiness, as in "Aquinas's treatise on beatitude." When used in the latter way, "beatitude" will not be capitalized [Tr.].

2. All intratextual biblical quotations are taken from the *New Revised Standard Version,* copyright 1989, 1995 by the Division of Christian Education of the National Council of the Churches of Christ in the United States of America [Tr.].

picts St. Stephen's martyrdom as an imitation of Christ's Passion.

We can therefore say that the spirituality of martyrdom constitutes the first Christian spirituality. We must add, further, that it is the mother of all spiritualities proceeding from the Gospel, in the heart of the church, on account of the profound and determinative influence that it has had upon all subsequent schools of spirituality and upon the ideal of holiness. It represents the first model of Christian spirituality, formed in immediate contact with the Gospel.

Hence Father Louis Bouyer is right when he writes [that] "the importance of martyrdom in the spirituality of the early Church can hardly be overestimated. But it is not merely for that era in which so many martyrdoms took place that [martyrdom] holds exceptional prominence. Excepting the evidence from the New Testament, martyrdom carries more weight than any other factor in the establishment of Christian spirituality. It hardly bears mentioning that the fact of martyrdom, as well as the theology surrounding it, are both already present in the New Testament. And yet there are few examples where we can get so clear a glimpse of the doctrinal development that links itself to the entire experience of the Church in the world!"

It must be noted, however, that martyrological literature is no longer very fashionable today. It carries with it an affirmation of Christian character so strong that it seems to conflict with the current trend, which favors an acceptance of pluralism among divided Christians, diverse religions, and among all opinions generally. Yet intolerance is not yet dead in our world, including among those who highly advocate tolerance but do not abide those they categorize as "conservative," "dogmatic," "traditional," or "too submissive to authority." On this reckoning, the spirituality of martyrdom risks being disqualified in advance, even though the martyrs [themselves] endured the cruelest sufferings and insults with the sort of patience and gentleness we could all take as an example.

Actually, it would not be of much use to discuss the martyrs and their spirituality if we were not also willing to acquaint ourselves with the documents that treat [the topic], if we did not make the effort to grasp the Gospel message that they contain and to appreciate [this message's] relevance to our own time. It is to this end that we have written this book, [a book] that was originally the subject of a university course in which we experienced once again that the best way to learn is to teach. The following pages contain the results of that research and investigation.

In order to help the reader understand and benefit most fully from the spirituality of martyrdom, we shall first offer a reflection on required reading, in particular with regard to the literature on martyrdom. I was talking one day with an old colleague from Philosophy, who did not understand the difference between watching a football match on television and attending it at the stadium. He reasoned that one could see the game better on the small screen than in the stands, which one could hardly deny is true. But he did not perceive what is proper about "being there" in the stadium, with the unique experience this procures. Yet there is something even better than being a spectator: it is to be a player who not only attends the game but "*makes it be*," creating the event, and so inciting the advent of victory or defeat.

These three levels of presence at a football match, as at any other event, apply also to the reading of a martyr narrative. We can read it as a book of history or as a novel, sitting in our armchairs as we would watch television. But we can also give it more personal attention, trying, as they say, "to put ourselves into the characters' shoes," so as to establish a certain spiritual contact with the martyrs as if we were there at the circus or in the prison, where the martyrs suffered and talked among themselves. The story thus comes alive and begins to speak to us; it touches us, calls out to us, and can even exert a decisive influence on our lives. Yet we nevertheless remain only readers, and a book, well written as it may be, can never replace the reality that the martyrs actually lived out. They alone, even more than the players in the stadium, have experienced real stress, pain, and torment, endurance and confidence, and the joy to which a confession of faith in Christ can give rise. They alone, together with all those who accompanied them, were able to speak authentically. There is therefore an inevitable distance between the martyrs and us. Martyrdom entails a commitment and an experience that are very personal and that we can only imagine.

All the same, at the center of the experience of martyrdom is a testimony on behalf of the martyr's faith and love for Christ, which any one of us can hear and take to heart, and which can enter into our lives and render us actors in our turn, in our own situation, according to our own state of life. Even if we are not threatened with death in the Western countries, we are all [still] called to give witness to the Lord and to the Gospel in our daily actions and in our life in society.[3] It is there where the martyrs join us and become our models, our traveling companions who guide us and sustain us. They instruct us to respond without reserve to the Lord's call and exhort us to entrust to him our entire life "unto death." They teach us candor when making a stand for the truth that appears to us, so that our words and our conduct might say "yes, yes," and "no, no," as the Gospel instructs us. They also exhort us to remain gentle while under attack, to exercise the patience of charity to people who oppose us, even through injustice, wantonness, or slander. In the communion of the church, [the martyrs] invite us to prayer, where

3. In French, the word for testimony, *témoinage*, is taken from the word for witness, *témoin*. At times, Pinckaers plays off this close lexical relation in a way that does not come through fully in English translation. We have tried to be as consistent as possible in rendering *témoin* as "witness" and *témoinage* as "testimony," but there were times when the clarity and style of the original text demanded a rendering more in line with the close relation of the French terms [Tr.].

we will secretly meet the Lord and, like them, receive the power of his Spirit. Finally, they offer us a testimony of the profound power of Christian faith—in the life of the most humble, the confidence that [this faith] nourishes even in the midst of physical torment, a hope, too, that goes beyond death, and above all of the real presence of Christ's love in us, transcending all sentiment. Thus the martyr is to us nothing less than a witness of Christ, convincing us to become witnesses in our turn in our own lives, just as he was before the judges and even after his death.

As for the question of pluralism, it seems to us that the testimony of the martyrs carries us beyond our intellectual debates and problems and takes on a universal human significance on account of the total commitment it entails, [a commitment given with] body and soul, which is a force capable of touching the heart of every person who hears aright, regardless of any division or divergence of opinion. As such, martyrdom can serve as one of the strongest catalysts of unity.

If we look back upon the history of Christianity, we can see in martyrdom the deepest and most reliable explanation of the extraordinary growth of the church in its first centuries. We can even say that martyrdom constituted, in its time, a concentration of spiritual energy so strong that it acted like a charge of dynamite, blowing away all obstacles, including the opposition of imperial Roman power, and provoking a most unexpected success.

As C. H. Dodd writes, "Having begun as an insignificant group within Judaism, [the Christian Church,] within a decade, burst its boundaries and appeared, at least in principle, 'catholic' or universal. Within the space of a generation, it was already strong enough in Rome, the metropolis of the universal Empire, to attract the unwelcome attention of the government. In two centuries, it had become a vast international institution, which stood up to the power of the empire that strove to destroy it, but would eventually admit defeat. In a little more than three centuries, Christianity would absorb the empire, and would go on to serve as the framework of medieval civilization.... The emergence of the Church in the first century is a historical phenomenon of the first order."

Certainly the foremost cause of the early church's expansion was the preaching of the apostles: the *kerygma*, the announcement of the good news of the coming of the Kingdom of God by Jesus, the Messiah foretold by the prophets, together with the Gospel narrative expounding his teachings, his passion, his death for all, his resurrection, and his ascension to the Father. After that would follow the sending of the Holy Spirit, who called all to a new life governed by the new commandment of brotherly love extending even unto the love of enemies. Yet this message, as original and compelling as it was with the signs and wonders accompanying it, would not have overpowered the philosophical and religious doctrines that then held sway in the Greco-Roman cultural world, if it had not culminated in the martyrdom of its exponents, beginning with the apostles, who reproduced in their death the sacrifice of Christ and thus confirmed by their blood the proclamation of the resurrection and the gift of the Spirit.

Martyrdom is therefore more than [just a] seal crowning the preaching of the apostles and Christian missionaries. It transforms their speech into a seed containing the sap of the Holy Spirit, which takes root in the hearts of believers and makes them fertile for future harvests. Such is the insight conveyed by the famous adage of Tertullian: "the blood of martyrs is the seed of Christians." In reality, the saying was crafted from a phrase in his *Apology*: "*Semen est sanguis christianorum*" (the blood of Christians is a seed).[4]

4. Unless otherwise marked, all quotations from patristic sources are taken from the Early Church Fathers series, originally edited by Philip Schaff. This passage is from chap. 50 of Tertullian's *Apology*, translated by Sydney Thelwall, in vol. 3 of the *Ante-Nicene Fathers* [Tr.].

Tertullian writes it in an address to the persecuting magistrates: "kill us, torture us, condemn us, grind us to dust; your injustice is the proof that we are innocent. Therefore God suffers that we thus suffer.... The oftener we are mown down by you, the more in number we grow; *the blood of Christians is seed*.... On this account it is that we return thanks on the very spot for your sentences. As the divine and human are ever opposed to each other, when we are condemned by you, we are acquitted by the Highest."[5] One finds the same idea a little later in the writings of Lactantius (260–325): "Christians cannot be diminished by persecution, because if their blood is seed, the growth promised to the faithful will be all the greater, as an abundant harvest leads to a yet more abundant yield."[6]

The idea of the fecundity of the blood of martyrs is clearly inspired by the Lord's words as reported by St. John: "unless a grain of wheat falls into the earth and dies, it remains just a single grain; but if it dies, it bears much fruit." (Jn 12:24). It links the martyrdom of Christians to the Passion of Christ in which this saying of Jesus is first realized, after which it comes to fruition in the members of his mystical Body who are submitted to a similar condemnation and agony. The martyrdom of Christians perpetuates the Passion [in its own mode] just as much as the Eucharist does sacramentally.[7] Therein lies the power of its influence.

Such was the experience of the first centuries. The principal engine of Christian expansion within the Roman empire was the spiritual energy of the faith in Jesus that was best demonstrated by

5. Tertullian, *Apology*, chap. 50.

6. Thus far we have not been able to locate the source of this quotation, which Pinckaers attributes to Lactantius [Tr.].

7. We have inserted "in its own mode" here to supply the corresponding adverbial phrase that would correspond with "sacramentally," but that Pinckaers's original manuscript does not supply [Tr.].

the martyrs, who became witnesses not only in word but in that supreme act performed by men and women of every origin, age, and condition: namely, that of accepting a tortuous death. We find here all the elements of Jesus' Passion, all the outlines of the scandal of the cross. Taking after their Master, as stated in the hymn [St. Paul quotes] to the *Philippians*, the martyrs made themselves "obedient to the point of death—even death on a cross"; therefore God exalted them also, and willed to exercise through them a decisive spiritual influence that extended, alongside the Gospel, to the furthest reaches of the earth and of [human] history. Their power came less from human courage, comparable to that of the other ancient heroes Tertullian evokes in *Ad martyras*, than from a humble faith in Christ, who manifested his strength through them, thus adding to their sacrifice a new communal dimension: even while publicly scorned and neglected in prison, they suffered as members of the Body of Christ, in communion with the church. And so their testimony is still able to resound today in the liturgy of the church: an appeal to all and an illustration of the greatest of the beatitudes: "Blessed are you ... when they persecute you ... on account of me. Rejoice and be glad!"

Thus the martyrs invite us, in our turn, to bear witness to our faith in Christ with intelligence and patience, faithfully and proudly, relying on the grace of the Spirit and on prayer more than on our own abilities and resources, whether personal or technical. [They invite us to bear witness] through every difficulty, contradiction, temptation, and humiliation that we may encounter, so that we too may prove to be good servants of divine Providence in the present world, good seeds planted in the soil of God for future harvests.

I

AN OVERVIEW OF THE SPIRITUALITY OF MARTYRDOM

In this chapter, we will first specify the meaning of the term "spirituality"; then we will take a brief sweeping look at the spirituality of martyrdom.

I. THE MEANING OF THE TERM AND CONCEPT OF "SPIRITUALITY"

We could easily entitle this first part "the martyrdom of spirituality" on account of all the divisions that have occurred within Christian spirituality, as well as the impoverishment of the terminology that one finds throughout its history.

According to the dictionary definition, the term "spirituality" has three meanings:

1. Metaphysical term. An attribute of whatever is spirit ... *the spirituality of the soul.*

2. Term of devotion. Anything relating to the interior exercises of a soul freed from the senses, which only seeks to perfect itself in the eyes of God ... *the new spirituality, the mysticism of Madam Guyon and de Fénelon.*

3. Generally, the character of whatever transcends matter and sense.... "It is still to Christianity that we owe this perfected sentiment (of love); which, seeking incessantly to purify the heart, was able to inject spirituality into the inclination which seemed least disposed to it."[1]

Historically, the second meaning is a product of modernity, dating back to the seventeenth century. It was first used to refer to Fénelon's mysticism, with a pejorative tint, which it fortunately lost through the frequency of its use. Before that, theologians regularly used the terms "mystical theology," "mystical asceticism," and simply "mysticism."

At present, the term "spirituality" is more akin to the expressions "spiritual life" or "interior life," which we use to differentiate from other dimensions, such as professional, social, or political life. Spirituality may thus be defined as the cultivation of religious sentiment, an account of interior progress based on a collection of principles, methods, practices, and exercises aimed at the acquisition of personal perfection before God. "Spirituality" becomes divided into different currents or schools according to the various conceptions of the spiritual life and the methods employed. We may point out, for example, Ignatian spirituality, which, with its "Exercises," has played a decisive role in the modern application of the term; "Franciscan spirituality"; "Dominican spirituality"; and "Salesian spirituality."

This conception of spirituality has become standard. It has entered into theological curricula with the distinction between dog-

1. Chateaubriand, *Génie* II.III.2.

matic theology, moral theology, biblical studies, and spirituality, and it has been inscribed in the titles of standard texts and reference works, such as *The History of Spirituality* and *The Dictionary of Spirituality*.

Critique of the Modern Term "Spirituality"

The Problems

This conception of spirituality presents serious problems:

1. It does not harmonize with the broader Christian tradition expressed in the writings of the fathers of the church and the great scholastics, for whom theology is fundamentally unified: at once theological, spiritual, exegetical, and pastoral. By separating dogmatics and ethics, this modern understanding [of the term] brings about a significant narrowing of perspective. Thus the various categories in which spirituality appears in the modern context are inevitably too narrow to account for the full spiritual richness of scripture and the works of the fathers and great scholastics. When applied to these authors, the division between moral and ascetical theology [on the one hand] and mysticism and spirituality [on the other] is anachronistic, an artificial imposition of boundaries that they did not presume.

2. The division into multiple schools of spirituality leads to a predominant focus upon differentiation at the risk of neglecting their common evangelical and ecclesial roots. They can thus appear as isolated cliques, whose rivalry undermines their insertion into the communion and unity of the church. It is therefore appropriate to reiterate the common root and foundation of Christian spirituality as a whole—namely, the Gospel. As for the spirituality of martyrdom, it does not represent one tiny spirituality among others; rather, it is written in the very heart of the Gospel. One may thus find its inspiration very much alive and at work throughout the many spiritual families.

3. The eighteenth and nineteenth centuries in particular have given to Catholic spirituality a psychological and individual orientation that has sequestered it from other dimensions of human life, most notably from the social and communal dimension, whether it is in the context of the church or the city. We have also associated spirituality too closely with practices of personal piety and particular devotions. Certainly, the spiritual life has its center in the innermost part of the human person, but it is [also] a source of inspiration that should animate every action, going beyond the sentiments and external practices of religion.

Reasons for This Narrowing of Perspectives Regarding Spirituality

One can best account for the relative narrowness of the perspectives of spirituality in the modern era by considering three historical phenomena, of which we can only make mention here but that we must acknowledge if we want to work toward a correction [of this tendency] and a broadening of our perspective.

1. Starting in the fourteenth century, a distinction was made between theology and mysticism or spirituality. At that time, the theology taught in the universities became more and more speculative. It was articulated according to rational procedures and the scholastic method and was expressed in technical and abstract language. It became the work and the domain of professional theologians. From that point, theology progressively distinguished itself from mysticism, which emerged from the experience of spiritual realities revealed in the life of faith and prayer, and which expressed those realties in a common concrete language, often with a highly emotional resonance. Mysticism is the work of Christian men and women moved by the love of God, sharing what they have experienced and discovered in order to help other Christians move and advance in the ways of God. Examples of [practitioners

of] this kind of mysticism include John Tauler and Henry Suso from the Rheinland, Catherine of Siena and Bridget of Sweden among women, and the Flemish mysticism of John Ruysbroeck and Thomas à Kempis, with his *Imitation of Christ*.

2. After the Council of Trent and particularly beginning in the seventeenth century, Catholic morality separated itself from that which came to be called "asceticism" or "mysticism" and began to focus more exclusively on the idea of obligation. Henceforth the moral domain would be circumscribed by the law and the commandments, which imposed fixed obligations on all Christians. Asceticism was reserved for those (namely, the consecrated) who sought after a higher mode of perfection by exercising the virtues and following the evangelical counsels. Mysticism came to imply special graces and indeed was rendered suspect by the extraordinary phenomena that often accompanied it. Spirituality would henceforth locate itself predominantly within the realm of asceticism. It would come to constitute a distinct and rather marginal subdivision of morality applicable only to an elite few. St. Francis de Sales was reacting against this conception of spirituality when he strove to place the devout or spiritual life within the reach of all the faithful.

3. The Protestant reformation had the effect, among Catholics, of removing from the people any direct, sustained contact with scripture, whose wealth no longer reached them except through selected fragments or by means of devotional books, hence the need and the success of particular devotions and spiritual books intended to feed religious sentiment, which were all the more necessary since the use of Latin barred, to some extent, the access to the liturgy.

A Broader Conception of Spirituality

Would it be too audacious to seek out a remedy to the various problems that we have just enumerated by broadening the perspectives of spirituality? In order to do that, we must first return to the New Testament itself, to St. Paul, for instance, and to see how he conceived of the spiritual life. In doing so, we will be reaching back to the very time in which the spirituality of martyrdom was born.

We take spirituality to refer to the study of the Christian life and its development insofar as [that life] is placed under the direction of the Holy Spirit. For Paul, the Christian life is life according to the Spirit: "If we live by the Spirit, let us also be guided by the Spirit" (Gal 5:25). "For the law of the Spirit of life in Christ Jesus has set you free from the law of sin and of death.... For those who live according to the flesh set their minds on the things of the flesh, but those who live according to the Spirit set their minds on the things of the Spirit" (Rom 8:2, 5). The Christian virtues are the fruits of the Spirit: "the fruit of the Spirit is love, joy, peace, patience, kindness, generosity, faithfulness, gentleness, and self-control" (Gal 5:22–23). "Spirituality" then describes the growth of the new man (Col 3:9–10), the interior man (Eph 3:16; 2 Cor 4:16).

For St. Paul, the Christian life is simply life according to the Spirit and encompasses the entire moral life. This, indeed, is how the *Catechism of the Catholic Church* presents Christian morality, placing it under the title "The vocation of man: life in the Spirit" (*CCC* §1669) and culminating its chapter on the virtues with a treatment of the gifts and fruits of the Holy Spirit (*CCC* §§1830–32). Christian morality therefore merits the designation "spirituality" insofar as it proceeds from the action of the Holy Spirit, which is its primary origin.

At the same time [though], the Christian or spiritual life is for St. Paul a *life in Christ*, a life incorporated into the mystical Body of Christ, open to the wealth of his mystery (Rom 14:7–8). In the First Letter to the Corinthians (chaps. 12–13), the spiritual gifts receive their measure and value to the extent that they are ordered to the building up of the one Body of Christ, the Church, through the operation of charity and the Spirit. In [Paul's] letters to the Colossians and Ephesians the description of the Christian life is placed under the guidance of the mystery of Christ, which he characterizes in two formulas: "in him the whole fullness of deity dwells bodily" (Col 2:9), and "that you may be filled with all the fullness of God" (Eph 3:19). We see here the two extreme points of the mystery of Christ: the body of the Lord—through which he became a human being like us, suffered and rose again, and into which we are mysteriously incorporated—and the divine glory manifested in the Resurrection, which bestows upon us a new life "hidden in Christ," which is life according to the Spirit.

Here again the *Catechism of the Catholic Church* follows St. Paul in entitling its third section on morality "Life in Christ" (*CCC* §1691ff.).

The spirituality of St. Paul is therefore a spirituality of Christ and the Holy Spirit, which draws together the entire Christian life and joins it, as a direct consequence, to the mystery of God revealed in Christ, which is the central focus of dogmatic theology.

In this way, spirituality extends and meets dogmatic theology. It is intimately and vitally connected to doctrine, to ethics, and to the study of the word of God. It is a dimension of all theology rather than some distinct theological subdiscipline.

We can nevertheless identify spirituality [as a discrete category] by characterizing this principal trait: [spirituality] is the study of the Christian life insofar as it is placed under the direction of the Holy Spirit. This [action of the Spirit] implies both a light that uncovers the mystery of Christ and an impulse that incorporates Christians into the mystical body of Christ through conformity to his life so that "the new man" takes on form in them.

This conception of spirituality allows us to transcend the particularism of diverse spiritualities, or rather to consider them all from the perspective of the primary origin that reveals their organic unity.

Different spiritualities have indeed been created and shaped by the Holy Spirit throughout the history of the church, as fruits of the Gospel proclamation. They receive their authentic value from this common source and should always be considered in relation to it, just as charisms remain the gifts of the one Spirit, according to St. Paul. Thus one might speak of a "communion of spiritualities" as one speaks of a "communion of saints," implying a community of origin and inspiration, a convergence and interpenetration that are more important than their differences.

It is from this perspective that we consider the spirituality of martyrdom not as a particular spirituality proper to the first centuries of the church or in a time of emergency, but as the evangelical spirituality that took shape in apostolic times and has [henceforth] become a model for subsequent spiritualities.

Our Method

One might think of a curriculum on the spirituality of martyrdom as a historically based study of the texts it has produced and a systematic analysis of their development through time and of their doctrine. That is the way we would proceed in patristics or if we were to compose a history or dictionary of spirituality. We must of course take account of and profit by such studies and presentations. [These works provide] a necessary foundation. Yet a book of spirituality has its [own] proper perspective. If it is true that the term "spirituality" derives from "spirit," then the goal of such a work will be to help the reader to penetrate into the heart of the historical texts in order to establish contact, through the text and dogma, with the spirit that constitutes the spirituality of a person, community, or era, describing it and even rendering it communicable, insofar as it is possible. It is an idealistic aim, to be sure, but a proper aim nonetheless of any treatment of spirituality that intends to get at the heart of the matter.

We therefore make use in this work of all the documents and studies available to us for the sake of our primary aim: to provide an entrée into texts that express the spirituality of martyrdom, by helping the reader penetrate beyond the surface of these texts so as to acquire a thorough and living comprehension of their subject matter. We are concerned with understanding not only simply the way in which martyrdom was for Christians an ordeal that they endured with patience when it was imposed upon them, but rather why it became in their eyes an expression of evangelical perfection and the object of a spiritually profound and characteristically Christian aspiration.

II. THE SPIRITUALITY OF MARTYRDOM

The text of Fr. Louis Bouyer, which we have cited earlier, invites us to take a brief initial look at the spirituality of martyrdom so as to measure its dimensions. The spirituality of martyrdom is the first fruit of the Gospel in the history of the church. It emerges directly from the times of the apostles and occupies the first three centuries of the patristic age. We can best approach it by a threefold consideration of:

1. Its rootedness in the Gospel;
2. Its importance to the early church; [and]
3. Its influence on the subsequent history of the church.

The Spirituality of Martyrdom and the Gospel

We cannot here attempt an exegetical study on the theme of persecution and martyrdom; however, it would be appropriate to cast a glance at some passages of scripture that deal with it.

The Importance of the Beatitude of the Persecuted

Let us begin then with the final Beatitude, that of the persecuted, which we find in Matthew 5:10–12 and in Luke 6:22–23.

At first glance, this Beatitude seems to be added on at the end like an appendix and to hold only relative importance for us. Whereas the other Beatitudes evoke situations and themes that concern us directly and generally—poverty, suffering, meekness and mercy, justice and peace—this Beatitude refers to a special situation of oppression that we no longer know in our land. It therefore appears less actualizable.

But, when we look more closely, we see that the last Beatitude is perhaps the most important, in the sense that it is the one toward which the others converge as toward their summit.[2] We can already see an indication of the last Beatitude's importance according to St. Matthew in the repetition of the fundamental promise of the Kingdom that he makes both there and in the first Beatitude (a literary technique known as *inclusio*), thus demonstrating the importance of this promise for all the Beatitudes. Furthermore, the Beatitude of the persecuted is the only one that receives a commentary, whose peculiarity is that it takes on a personal voice: "Blessed are you when men revile and persecute *you* ... because of *me*. Rejoice and be glad."

But above all the Beatitude of the persecuted reveals to us the historical and personal context of the evangelists as well as the first-century Christians for whom they wrote: a situation of perse-

2. Note that we approach the text of the Beatitudes here just as our Gospels present it to us, leaving aside the question of formation and successive redactions, as well as the question of the extent to which and the terms in which Jesus might have pronounced a Beatitude evoking with such precision a situation of the church after his death. Indeed, we consider the Beatitudes here insofar as they are the historical basis for the spirituality of martyrdom found in the early church, and are built upon the Gospels themselves.

cution on account of their relationship to Christ. Here is the reason this Beatitude takes on a universal importance: the Beatitudes in their entirety, and even the Gospels and epistles, must be read and understood in light of this aspect of Christian life and must take into account its particular flavor.

The orientation of the Beatitudes toward the persecuted is especially clear in Luke, where the Beatitudes number only four. Dom Dupont concurs with the opinion of Schürmann on this topic.[3] Apart from the literary and exegetical arguments, it is certain that the concrete life context created by the preaching of the Gospel and by the antagonistic, often violent reaction it elicited gives a special coloration to the other Beatitudes: persecution provokes a certain experience of poverty, hunger, suffering, and weeping that assumes its own proper place and significance from the fact that it comes at the hands of the public authority and that it is endured for the sake of Christ.

Can we then extend this prevailing consciousness of persecution to the particular Beatitudes of Matthew dealing with mercy, purity of heart, and peacemaking? It would seem so. The meek are those who suffer patiently the violence of persecution, while the merciful [are those who] refuse to avenge themselves and pardon the injustice that is done to them. As for the pure of heart, they guard themselves from being contaminated by the hatred that others bear toward them, and [lastly] the peacemakers are those who continue to seek peace even as others make war on them. This special coloration in no way prevents each of the Beatitudes from having its own proper content and nuance in a more peaceful context.

We should also note that the persecution against the followers of Jesus went through two historical stages: persecution by the

3. Jacques Dupont, *Les Béatitudes,* tome 3, *Les évangélistes,* Études bibliques, 78–79 (Paris: Gabalda, 1973).

synagogue, followed by persecution at the hands of the secular authorities. The Gospel itself indicates this distinction: "Beware of them, for they will hand you over to councils and flog you in their synagogues; and you will be dragged before governors and kings because of me, as a testimony to them and the Gentiles" (Mt 10:17–18).

It seems that, for his part, St. Luke is thinking predominantly about persecution in the synagogue.[4] This persecution itself passed through two stages: during the time of Jesus and then after Jesus' death. We will leave to specialists the task of distinguishing these different stages according to the Gospel texts and their sources.

The Christian Soul in Persecution

The most important thing for us is to identify and understand what the final Beatitude says about the characteristic mark of the Christian soul in the midst of persecution. One would expect Christians to be overwhelmed by fear or rebellion or that they would take on the mentality of the hunted, like all the world's persecuted peoples. But the quality that predominates among them is rather a peaceful and triumphant joy: "Rejoice and be glad, for your reward is great in heaven."

The vigor of this joy appears all the stronger insofar as it is born out of a paradox that is at once powerful and realistic. Insult, calumny, persecution with its threats and its injustices are among the most painful experiences one can have. [These experiences] also include the serious danger of scandal, since it is the very preaching of the Gospel that provokes persecution as the categorical refusal of the people and the authorities. What results is the temptation to doubt the Gospel message amid the intense pressure of public opinion. Persecution is the great test of faith, evoked by the last petition of the *Our Father*: "Lead us not into

4. See ibid., 3:333.

temptation, but deliver us from evil." Jesus would also say to Peter, "Simon, Simon, listen! Satan has demanded to sift all of you like wheat, but I have prayed for you that your own faith may not fail" (Lk 22:31–32). Yet it is within this test that the victorious joy of the disciples bursts forth: they suffer on account of Christ and discover in that very persecution a sure way to the Kingdom of heaven, a guarantee of its future possession. Pierre Bonnard rightly notes that joy in martyrdom finds its technical expression in the final Beatitude,[5] whose invitation to joy (*agalliasthe*) is highlighted especially in the First Letter of St. Peter: "In this you rejoice, even if now for a little while you have had to suffer various trials, so that the genuineness of your faith—being more precious than gold that, though perishable, is tested by fire—may be found to result in praise and glory and honour when Jesus Christ is revealed" (1 Pt 1:6–7). Likewise it says, "Beloved, do not be surprised at the fiery ordeal that is taking place among you to test you, as though something strange were happening to you. But rejoice in so far as you are sharing Christ's sufferings, so that you may also be glad and shout for joy when his glory is revealed. If you are reviled for the name of Christ, you are blessed, because the spirit of glory, which is the Spirit of God, is resting on you" (1 Pt 4:12–14).

One can also recognize in the Beatitudes different aspects and qualities of the soul of the persecuted Christian: an acceptance (even to the point of a love) of poverty for Christ; meekness in the face of violence; patience in affliction and consolation from God; hunger and thirst for justice and interior satisfaction; mercy, kindness when under attack and pardon of offenses while imploring divine mercy; the purity of heart that preserves one from the hatred of others and so allows one to approach God so as to see him; [and] peace of heart amid the thick of battle, bestowing an

5. Pierre Bonnard, *L'évangile selon saint Matthieu*, 2nd ed. (Neuchâtel: Editions Labor et Fides, 1970), 58.

abiding awareness of being a child of God—such are the various manifestations of joy and corresponding foretastes of the promised reward.[6]

The Interpretation of St. Augustine and St. Thomas

We insert here a remark on the interpretation of the Beatitudes given by St. Augustine (*Commentary on the Sermon on the Mount*) and St. Thomas (*Commentary on Matthew, ST* I-II, q. 69). In their commentaries these two masters also place the Beatitude of the persecuted at the summit of the evangelical Beatitudes, as their culmination, but [they do so] for reasons different than those that we have indicated, reasons that depend upon their interpretation [of the Beatitudes] as a whole.

Both, indeed, organize the Beatitudes according to a progressive ascent. St. Augustine, inspired by the experience he recounts in the *Confessions*, reads the first seven Beatitudes as an outline of seven degrees of the spiritual life, beginning with conversion in humility and poverty and eventually leading to peace and wisdom. The eighth Beatitude, for its part, recapitulates and portrays all the foregoing Beatitudes, displaying their full achievement and perfection. In addition, in the meditation on preparatory texts for his preaching, Augustine had the idea of associating the Beatitudes with the seven gifts of the Holy Spirit, since one cannot travel the path that they trace without the grace of the Spirit. Later, in his commentary on the sermon, it will occur to him to note a correspondence with the seven petitions of the *Our Father* as well, since it is prayer that obtains for us the aid of the Spirit. Augustine's commentary is a little symphony of catechesis and spirituality, set to the meter of the number seven, the sign of perfection.

6. The phrase at the end of this paragraph was originally written *before* "an acceptance (even to the point of a love) of poverty." We have placed it here for the sake of clarity and coherence of expression [Tr.].

Yet herein we see one of the most likely explanations for his setting aside of the eighth Beatitude, which remains without parallel among the gifts of the Holy Spirit or the petitions of the *Our Father*. We see in his interpretation of the Beatitudes a reflection of all the spiritual teaching and experience of St. Augustine, from the humility that conforms us to the incarnate Word to the wisdom that conforms us to the word of God and so places us under the movement of the Holy Spirit and of grace.

St. Thomas, who clearly knows St. Augustine's classic commentary well and used it in the *Summa theologiae*, nevertheless gives us an original interpretation [of the Beatitudes] in accordance with the account of genuine happiness he develops in his treatise on beatitude (*ST* I-II, q. 1–5), [a treatise] that serves as the foundation of his moral thought. For him the Beatitudes are divided, according to the three responses that philosophers have given to the question of happiness.

The first three Beatitudes dismiss conceptions of happiness rooted in the sensible order: through the first riches and honor [are dismissed]; through the second, the desire to dominate, which is connected to the irascible appetite; and through the third the lure of pleasures associated with the concupiscible appetite. Their countervailing virtues are humility, courage, and temperance.

The fourth and fifth Beatitudes concern conceptions of happiness centered on exterior action. They are not bad per se, but they remain insufficient nonetheless: the fourth Beatitude addresses action governed by justice, according to what is due, while the fifth touches upon action embodying liberality or mercy.

The sixth and seventh Beatitudes focus on the conceptions of happiness rooted in contemplation and love, which, although good in themselves, can never be perfectly realized here below. The sixth Beatitude deals with moral action oriented toward interior purity, [while] the seventh addresses the effect of moral action upon one's neighbors, which is to say, peace. [These Beatitudes] align themselves with the intellectual virtues: the practical with prudence and the contemplative with wisdom. The eighth Beatitude confirms and illustrates them all, taken together as a whole.

At the same time, St. Thomas follows St. Augustine in establishing a close link between the Beatitudes and the gifts of the Holy Spirit, which [St. Thomas] treats in question 68 of the *prima secundae*. For him, the Beatitudes are, alongside gifts, which are associated with the virtues, an essential component of Christian action. St. Thomas reveals his conception of the moral life in his interpretation of the Beatitudes. Or better yet, looking at it the other way around, we might say that the Sermon on the Mount serves as a guiding light for his theological investigation into Christian life and experience.

The Beatitude of the persecuted is predominant [in Thomas] not as the concrete context of Christian life, nor as the cause of any decisive achievement or coloration—that is, as a principle of interpretation for the other Beatitudes—but as the summit toward which the Christian life ascends, fixed upon the promises of the sixth and seventh Beatitudes: the beatific vision, wisdom and peace, or the contemplation and the peacemaking love of God. With St. Augustine and St. Thomas we are already beyond the historical era of the spirituality of martyrdom. The ideal of martyrdom, understood concretely, gives way to the ideal of contemplative and loving wisdom, though [the former] remains very much assumed.

The Context of Persecution Illuminates the Church

Let us return to the Beatitudes of the Gospel. If it is true that the last Beatitude describes to us the life context of the sacred authors and their recipients, [then] [this Beatitude] allows us to better understand the Gospels themselves and helps to explain the somewhat harsh and straightforward character of some of Christ's sayings and directives. The point comes across with particular clarity in the second part of the apostolic discourse: "Beware of them, for they will hand you over to councils and flog you in their synagogues; and you will be dragged before governors and kings because of me, as a testimony to them and the Gentiles" (Mt 10:17–18). The context of persecution, described in detail, allows us to understand the words already quoted: "Do not think that I have come to bring peace to the earth; I have not come to bring peace, but a sword.... Whoever welcomes you welcomes me, and whoever welcomes me welcomes the one who sent me" (Mt 10:34–47). These words will appear later as conditions for becoming a disciple, in connection with the first prediction of the Passion, indicating the culmination of the persecution against Jesus: "If any want to become my followers, let them deny themselves and take up their cross and follow me" (Mt 16:24).

One could therefore say that, as a whole, the Gospel is a manual of combat. It is written for disciples fighting to proclaim the word of Christ before adversaries who do not refrain from employing the harshest possible methods. Nonetheless they continue the struggle, with souls and sentiments resembling those described in the Beatitudes. There is no doubt that certain Gospel passages, such as the parable of the murderous tenants, more directly presuppose a time of persecution, but they all stand out in a particular way when read from this perspective. It is within this perspective that they were read and understood by the first Christians.

Persecution and Spiritual Combat

Placing the Gospel within a context of persecution must not estrange it from those of us for whom such an experience is rare and seems remote. The Gospel exists and can be understood at different levels. It is situated externally within an external, sociological, and historical context, which is usually what comes to mind when one first thinks of persecution. But at the same time, it reveals [persecution] to be rooted in a more profound and basic dimension: the spiritual plane, where the human heart faces God. Here, persecution becomes spiritual combat—combat between Jesus and the spirit of evil who instigates rejection and persecution; [combat] between the gospel Word and the evil instincts that impede its growth in the human heart.

On this plane, persecution against the Gospel takes place in the soul of every person who hears the call of the Word with its demands.[7] It exerts itself in the division and contention between the Holy Spirit and the flesh, as St. Paul puts it in his Letter to the Galatians (Gal 5:16ff). Thus all the texts of the Gospel that directly or indirectly presuppose persecution can perfectly well apply to us. They warn us that, even if we enjoy religious freedom outwardly, we cannot interiorly fall asleep, since we are all subject to the oppositions and temptations of spiritual combat: "Be careful then how you live, not as unwise people but as wise, making the most of the time, because the days are evil. So do not be foolish, but understand what the will of the Lord is" (Eph 5:15–17). [These texts] teach us to conduct this necessary spiritual combat with the same vigor as the first Christians, who resisted their Jewish and pagan adversaries. They are like trumpets of war that warn us not to rely on impressions and illusions of a facile peace, or on the promises of prophets announcing a false tranquility. Again, in the words of St. Paul, one who experienced persecution in all its forms, "Put on the whole armour of God, so that you may be able to stand against the wiles of the devil. For our struggle is not against enemies of

7. We have translated Pinckaers's term *homme* here as "person" instead of the more literal "man" so as better to keep with contemporary conventions regarding the use of the male pronoun for general reference. We do not believe the replacement in this case obscures the intended meaning in any way [Tr.].

blood and flesh, but against the rulers, against the authorities, against the cosmic powers of this present darkness, against the spiritual forces of evil in the heavenly places" (Eph 6:10–12). In this way the spirituality of martyrdom has been appropriated in other contexts by subsequent Christian spiritualities.

One may indeed read the Beatitudes as the description of spiritual combat between the flesh and the Spirit, between the evil tendencies in us and the action of God's grace. The first Beatitude addresses the tendency toward possession; it exhorts detachment and poverty, pointing the way to interior freedom. The second Beatitude attacks the tendency toward anger and violence by means of meekness and self-mastery, which soothe us. The third Beatitude counters the tendency toward pleasure and promises interior consolation, the joy that comes from God. The fourth Beatitude transforms hunger and thirst into a desire for justice and a yearning for God and nourishes us like solid food. The fifth Beatitude reduces the tendency toward vengeance by conveying to us the mercy of God, teaching us to exercise it to the point where we are able to enjoy it. The sixth Beatitude takes aim at impurity and duplicity, aiming to produce a limpidity of heart transparent to the radiance of spiritual light. The seventh Beatitude then combats the tendency toward aggression and domination; it promises us an active participation in the peace of God. Finally, the eighth Beatitude diminishes our rebellion against the injustice done to us because of Christ and gives us the strength and joy to suffer for him.

The Authenticity of the Beatitude of the Persecuted

We have here the beginning of a response to an exegetical problem: could Christ have pronounced the Beatitude of the persecuted, when [this Beatitude] presupposes a context pertaining to the first generation of Christians, which did not materialize until after his death? Could not the last Beatitude be the work of the primitive community?

It is clear that the Beatitude of the persecuted and other Gospel texts that speak of persecution, such as the missionary discourse, are marked in their formulation by the experience of persecution endured by the Christian community after Jesus' death. But that in no way prevents these words and this teaching from having substantial continuity with those of Christ himself. As we have said, the essence of persecution resides in spiritual combat against the evil that is at work both outwardly and inwardly. Now, during his mortal life, Jesus engaged the forces and spirits of evil in a long battle, facing persecution from the leaders of the Jewish people that would [eventually] lead him to the cross. During his ministry, therefore, he was already living in a context of persecution, a context that allowed him to blossom in his teachings, especially as a premonition to his disciples, the Beatitude of the persecuted and guidance for times of trial. It is also appropriate to recognize in Jesus a special insight, surpassing the all-too-human views of his disciples and his adversaries, into the necessary confrontation with the spirit of evil in its resistance to the Gospel. [This confrontation] would lead to the Passion, which provides precisely the definitive model of the Christian understanding of martyrdom. Did he not on three occasions announce that very Passion to his disciples, who could not bear the thought?

It would also be appropriate to grant the early Christian community the freedom to express the teachings of Christ in the context of its own experience of the truth and the relevance of his prediction. We are dealing here not merely with dead words transmitted materially through books and libraries, but rather with living words that manifest their truth in the experience of their message and how it is accomplished in the life of Christians. These words are the seeds of life that grow so as to produce fruit—a fruit that may bear verbal coverings slightly different from the original seed.

The Old Testament Roots of the Beatitude of the Persecuted

It is fitting, finally, to take account of the way in which the last Beatitude is rooted in the Old Testament, as indicated by its very formulation: "For in the same way they persecuted the prophets who came before you." The most prominent of these predecessors is without doubt Jeremiah, who repeatedly expresses his lamentations under persecution. Christians will eventually take some of these texts and apply them directly to Jesus in his Passion: "But I was like a gentle lamb led to the slaughter. And I did not know it was against me that they devised schemes, saying, 'Let us destroy the tree with its fruit, let us cut him off from the land of the living, so that his name will no longer be remembered!'" (Jer 11:19ff; see also chaps. 26, 37 and 38.)

The book of Wisdom evinces the motif of persecution in a text that likewise inspires the Passion narrative: "Let us lie in wait for the righteous man, because he is inconvenient to us and opposes our actions ... for if the righteous man is God's child, he will help him, and will deliver him from the hand of his adversaries. Let us test him with insult and torture, so that we may find out how gentle he is, and make trial of his forbearance. Let us condemn him to a shameful death, for, according to what he says, he will be protected" (Ws 2:12, 18–20).

The theme is again found in the fourth song of the Servant of Yahweh, but with an explanation that clarifies the profound significance of persecution in the context of the work of redemption: persecution that causes the suffering of the just is a means that God uses to redeem men from their sins; it becomes the instrument of choice for redemption and reconciliation: "yet we accounted him stricken, struck down by God, and afflicted. But he was wounded for our transgressions, crushed for our iniquities; upon him was the punishment that made us whole, and by his bruises we are healed" (Is 53:4–5).

The book of Daniel, finally (Dn 7:24ff), gives voice to the eschatological character of persecution, in a perspective that will resume in the book of Revelation (Rv17:12ff).

Thus the Beatitude of the persecuted is the culmination of a grand prophetic theme in the Old Testament. It even receives, in Jeremiah, for instance, an illumination that relates it to the Passion of Jesus as the paradigmatic exemplification of the prophetic trial and at the same time the model of how Christians should endure persecution. Persecution leads the Christian disciple to reproduce in his life the Passion of Christ, which was prefigured by the sufferings of the prophets.

Conclusion

It is on this already well-developed evangelical foundation that the spirituality of martyrdom in the first three centuries will be built and, above all, lived out. If we want to understand it in depth and appreciate its riches, it is indispensable that we read in the light of the gospel texts those documents telling us of the martyrs of the first period of the church's history.

The Importance of the Spirituality of Martyrdom in the First Three Centuries of the Church

The spirituality of martyrdom dominated the first three centuries of the church's history. Certainly this period gave rise to works of theological and spiritual reflection on a grand scale, owing to the encounter of the Christian faith with the Greco-Roman culture. Such works include, in the second century, the *Didache* and the *Shepherd of Hermas*, *The Dialogue with Trypho* and the two *Apologies* of St. Justin, the *Adversus haereses* of St. Irenaeus; in the third century, the *Protrepticus*, the *Pedagogue*, and the *Stromata* of Clement of Alexandria, the *Peri Archon* of Origen (the first great theological synthesis), the corpus of Tertullian, and the works of St. Cyprian in Africa. An entire worldview, and thus a spirituality, unfolds itself in these works, particularly in the case of Origen.

Nonetheless, the ideal of martyrdom remains predominant. Most of these authors either experienced this persecution themselves or had direct encounters with it; above all, they recognized and proclaimed the preeminence of martyrdom for the Christian way of life.

Here is St. Ignatius of Antioch, writing during his voyage to Rome, where he would undergo martyrdom: "For I myself, though I am in chains and can comprehend heavenly things, the ranks of the angels and the hierarchy of principalities, things visible and invisible, for all this I am not yet a disciple" (*Letter to the Trallians* V.2).[8] "May I have the pleasure of the wild beasts that have been prepared for me.... I know what I need, I know it, myself.[9] Then I will truly be a disciple" (*Letter to the Romans* V.2 and IV.2).[10]

Several of these authors wrote about martyrdom as the supreme coronation of the Christian life: Origen, for instance—who himself ardently desired martyrdom and was tortured under Decius—in his *Exhortation to Martyrdom*; St. Cyprian in his *Letters to Confessors* (letters 6, 10–37, 76, 81) and *Exhortation to Martyrdom* addressed to Fortunatus; and Tertullian in his *Ad martyras*.

8. This quotation is taken from J. B. Lightfoot and J. R. Harmer's translation of St. Ignatius of Antioch's "Letter to the Trallians," in *The Apostolic Fathers*, edited by Michael W. Holmes, 2nd ed. (Grand Rapids, Mich.: Baker, 1991), 99 [Tr.].

9. It is unclear to what passage in the original text of St. Ignatius's *Letter to the Romans* the phrase "I know what I need, I know it, myself" corresponds [Tr.].

10. This quotation is taken from Lightfoot and Harmer's translation of St. Ignatius of Antioch's "Letter to the Romans," in *Apostolic Fathers*, 103–4.

This is all the more remarkable as this ideal of martyrdom finds no correspondence with the Greek frame of mind. While Greek thought tends toward the detachment from the body and the sensible world, martyrdom implies an essential participation of the body in Christian perfection to the extent that [such perfection] culminates in the giving of one's physical life for Christ in the sacrifice of the body. In this act the body is sanctified, as evidenced by the veneration of martyrs' relics. The Gnostics, for example, were condemned by the church primarily because of their rejection of martyrdom as useless.[11] Likewise, while Gnosticism, influenced by Greek philosophy, tended to form elite groups of initiates who enjoyed a superior knowledge and were called to a perfect life that separated them from the common faithful, the ideal of martyrdom remained open to all Christians indiscriminately as the supreme perfection of one's love for Christ. With perfect equality, the persecutions bring together bishops, deacons, the faithful, men and women, masters and slaves, to the same glorious death. We exult in the graces granted to even the weakest, such as the servant Blandina of Lyon.

Thus the spirituality of martyrdom overshadows other forms of spirituality throughout the first three centuries of the church. It is properly evangelical, since it is nourished directly by the Gospel and imposes itself because of [the Gospel] in the Greco-Roman world, which was not particularly prepared for it. Thus one can say that [the spirituality of martyrdom] is specifically Christian. One can observe this quality even in the etymology of the term: the sense of the [Greek] word *martus* is transformed by Christian parlance to the point that it acquires a new meaning, that of "witness," as we shall see further on.

11. See Henri Leclercq, *Dictionaire archaéologie chrétienne et de liturgie* (*DAL*), part 2, ed. Fernand Cabrol, Henri Leclercq, and Henri Irénée Marrou (Paris: Letouzey et Ané, 1931), 10:2453.

The Importance of the Spirituality of Martyrdom in the Subsequent History of the Church

Because the spirituality of martyrdom is linked to the historical fact of persecution by the bodily engagement it entails, it could not subsist in the same form within the church after the era of Roman persecution. Other forms of spirituality will emerge to take its place. The monastic, eremitic, and cenobitic spiritualities, which are at the origin of religious life, will come to dominate Christian spirituality until the thirteenth century alongside the Augustinian spirituality based on wisdom and charity, which will give birth among others, to the canonical life. And finally, the ideal of holiness would endure and spread throughout the church up to our own day.

Nevertheless, from their origins these spiritualities have kept a very close link to the ideal of martyrdom. As Father Bouyer writes, "The continuity between monasticism and martyrdom is evident on all points."[12] According to him, the asceticism of the New Testament, [originally] designed to prepare disciples for the return of Christ, comes to be seen in the ancient church as a preparation for martyrdom, since the persecutions remind Christians of the necessity of living in the world as though they did not belong to it as well as the reality of the spiritual warfare to be waged here below. This asceticism and this combat will prove to be easily transferable to monastic spirituality. The connection is accurate insofar as asceticism is equivalent to a spiritual combat. It bears remembering, however, that the love of Christ, which extends to the point of giving one's life, whether in martyrdom or through the consecration of one's entire life, is in both cases the most fundamental element.

12. Bouyer, *Histoire de la spiritualité* (Paris: Aubier, 1960), 1:260.

The Christian ideal of sanctity emerges directly from the spirituality of martyrdom. It was the martyrs who first received the title "saint" in the present sense of the word; they were the first ones to be elevated to the altars, and they received ecclesial veneration. In the history of the church, the saints are the direct successors of the martyrs. In the Roman canon, only the martyrs are still mentioned. The affiliation is so strong as to show in an evolution of vocabulary. The term *sanctus*, which in the classical language signifies a thing or a person set apart for God, attaches itself to the martyrs with a new and deeper religious meaning. As Fr. [Hippolyte] Delehaye writes, "From the moment it is reserved for martyrs, the meaning of the term (*sanctus*) changes radically, or rather acquires a precision that it lacked up to this point. The martyr is, *par excellence*, worthy of respect from the faithful, [and] the supreme mark of this respect is the homage of public veneration. From this point, 'saint' and 'object of veneration' come to be strictly synonymous. As a technical term, *sanctus* no longer has any other sense."[13] It is this new meaning, charged with Christian values, that would be transmitted from the martyrs to the confessors of later centuries.

Finally the ideal of martyrdom will live on in the Christian soul as a model, as a latent desire, if not as a form of nostalgia. Indeed, the martyr represents a particularly concrete, clear, and evocative form of the complete [self-]offering to Christ that is the basis of every authentically Christian spirituality. Hence St. Dominic and St. Teresa of Avila aspired to martyrdom in their own time.

III. THE DOCUMENTS

The literature dealing with the martyrs is very rich. It may be divided into several categories.

13. See Hippolyte Delehaye, *Essai sur le culte des saints dans l'antiquité* (Brussels: Société des Bollandistes, 1927), 8–59.

1. First there are the *Acta*, which reproduce the official minutes of the martyrs' interrogations, usually preceded by an introduction and concluded by an account of the execution. They are "the exact transcription, or nearly so, of the court minutes prepared by the pagans and sold to the faithful by the servants of the court."[14] Thus we have: the Acts of Justin and his companions (Rome, 165); the Acts of the martyrs of Sicilium in Africa (July 17, 180); the proconsular Acts of St. Cyprian (Carthage, September 14, 238), "the piece closest to the original, if not the original itself," as Henri Leclercq writes;[15] the martyrdom of Apollonius under Commodius (between 161 and 192); and the Acts of Ss. Carpus, Papylus, and Agathonice, under Marcus Aurelius (between 161 and 169).

2. The historical narratives or Passions are written by eyewitnesses or by other well-informed contemporaries, often with the help of transcripts. They include most notably: the death of the deacon Stephen in the Acts of the Apostles (6:8–8:3); the martyrdom of Polycarp of Smyrna, composed immediately after the event in 156;[16] the letter from the churches of Vienne and Lyon to the churches in Asia and Phrygia (177 or 178), inserted by Eusebius of Caesarea in his *Ecclesiastical History*, book V;[17] and the Passion of Perpetua and Felicity (Carthage, March 7, 203), which is partially an autobiography. One can find these texts as well as many others in the compilation entitled *The True Golden Legend*.[18]

3. There are also acts and passions that are fictitious to some degree, but nevertheless contain actual facts, which were frequent-

14. See *DAL*, part 2, 10:2475.

15. See *DAL*, part 2, 10:2480.

16. Edition in *Ignace d'Antioche, Polycarpe de Smyrne, Lettres, Martyre de Polycarpe.*, ed., trans. Pierre Thomas Camelot, 3rd ed.; Sources chrétiennes, no. 10. (Paris: Éditions du Cerf, 1958).

17. *Histoire ecclésiastique* II, livres V–VII, 4th ed., Greek text, translation and notes by Gustave Bardy, *Sources chrétiennes* 41 (Paris: Éditions du Cerf, 1994).

18. Paul Monceaux, *La vrai légende dorée* (Paris: Payot, 1928).

ly taken from ancient Acts. Take, for example, the Passion of the veteran Tipasius, or that of the actor Genesius. These documents date from the end of the fourth century through the fifth century.

4. Romantic or epic legends, such as the martyrdom of St. Cecilia and the martyrdom of the eleven thousand virgins, have abounded from the end of the fourth century up to the Middle Ages.

5. Finally, there are theological writings on martyrdom: the *Letters of St. Ignatius of Antioch*;[19] Tertullian's *Ad Martyras*;[20] Origen's *Exhortations to Martyrdom*;[21] and St. Cyprian's *Exhortation to Martyrdom Addressed to Fortunatus*[22] (before 241).

19. See *Ignace d'Antioch, Polycarpe du Smyrne*, in *Lettres, Martyr du Polycarpe*, trans. Pierre-Thomas Camelot, *Sources chrétiennes* 10 (Paris: Éditions du Cerf, 1969).

20. Tertullian, *Ad Martyras*, translated in *Sources* 4 (1978): 167–73.

21. Origen, *De la prière: Exhortation au martyre*, trans. Gustave Bardy (Paris: Librarie Lecoffre, J. Gabalda, 1931).

22. St. Cyprian, *Exhortation au martyre adressée à Fortunat*, trans. J. Boulet, in *Saint Cyprien, évêque de Cartilage et martyr* (Avignon: Aubanel, 1923); see Johannes Quasten, *Initiation aux Pères de l'Eglise* (Paris: Éditions du Cerf, 1966), 1:199stff.

2

THE DEFINITION OF MARTYRDOM

The Martyr Is a Witness

I. THE COMMON CONCEPTION OF MARTYRDOM

In modern language and representation, the concept of martyrdom revolves around the evocation of torture and death endured for Christian belief, for some religious conviction or other, or even for nonreligious convictions. Here, for example, are the definitions found in *Le Grand Robert* dictionary:

martyr: One who has suffered death for having refused to renounce the Christian faith; One who dies, who suffers in defense of a cause: *martyr of liberty, of science*; One who suffers much ill treatment: *to be someone's martyr.*

martyrdom: The death, torture and suffering which a martyr endures so as not to deny his faith; Death and suffering endured in defense of a cause; Cruel punishment, torment, great suffering: *the martyrdom of being separated, the lover's martyrdom*; A painful or unpleasant situation.

to martyr or ***make a martyr:*** to cause great suffering, *to martyr a child.*

Thus, apart from the words, the idea that evokes martyrdom for us is one that highlights the experience of torture and death. Christian paintings and literature have emphasized the portrayal of the torments endured by the martyrs to such an extent that the term has become practically synonymous with torture, and as a result other components of the concept, such as death itself, have been relegated to the background or neglected.

This accentuation of pain in the representation of martyrdom can inhibit us from entering into the spirituality of martyrdom as it was practiced by the first Christians and from understanding the principal evangelical element that gives it its significance and its spiritual richness, as well as its universal value.

The question before us, then, is: what is the first and principal element of Christian martyrdom? Is it the torture and death endured on account of one's faith and religious convictions? Is it not rather the witness given to Christ, so complete that it extends to the acceptance of death? The difference is important: if martyrdom is above all torment, suffering, and death, one can separate it from the cause for which one suffers, as a vessel may be separated from its contents. Christian martyrdom, then, is no longer distinguishable from any other martyrdom accepted on behalf of any other cause. But if the principal element of martyrdom lies beyond mere suffering and rests in the witness one gives to a cause for which one accepts even death, then the content, the reason for suffering, becomes the essence of martyrdom, and we can pinpoint what is specific to Christian martyrdom—namely, the witness on behalf of Christ and the Gospel, which is the source of the spirituality of martyrdom. In this way, the content determines the vessel and gives it its meaning.

II. THE MARTYR IS ESSENTIALLY A WITNESS

To uncover the primary element, the fundamental core of Christian martyrdom, one need only retrace the [etymological] evolution of the Greek terms *martus*, *marturia*, *marturion*, and *martureô* in the texts of the New Testament and the early church in order to arrive at their current meaning.

In Nonbiblical Greek

In common Greek, the term *martus* and those derived from it were mainly employed in the legal context, in the field of law, to mean *witness* or *testimony*, as in "to produce a witness" or "to call on the gods as witness." However, philosophical language introduces an important split in meaning, as evidenced by Aristotle's observation that while testimony is usually based on facts—events that are directly observed—it can also concern truths: ways of seeing of which the speaker is convinced, and [testimony can] be the manifestation of moral and philosophical convictions.

In the Septuagint

In the Septuagint, the term *martus* is employed in the usual Greek sense. To quote a passage from Isaiah, "Let them bring their witnesses to justify them, and let them hear and say, 'It is true.' You are my witnesses, says the Lord, and my servant whom I have chosen" (Is 43:9–10). God calls on Israel as a witness on his behalf before the nations. He invites them to testify to their experience of his divine activity in their past and present history. The goal is to bring Israel to a religious confession on behalf of their God.

We also encounter in the Old Testament, most notably in the second book of Maccabees, well-defined martyr figures such as Eleazar and the seven brothers (Mc 6–7), so that one can readily see them as predecessors of the Christian martyrs. Yet the term *martus* is never attributed to them, and the reason seems to be as follows: the Jewish martyrs live their fidelity to the Law till the end, their piety toward it, but they are not witnesses on behalf of a person, as the Christian martyrs are to Christ. As a result, nothing can be drawn from the Jewish idea of martyrdom to describe the formation of the ancient Christian concept or the evolution of the term *martus* that it has produced.

The New Testament

We encounter the classical use of the term *martus* and its derivations in many passages of the New Testament, [referring to] witnesses of certain facts before a tribunal. "Then the high priest tore his clothes and said, 'Why do we still need witnesses?'" (Mk 14:63). "They [also] set up false witnesses (against Stephen)" (Acts 6:13). Also, in Paul's speech before the people at Jerusalem, "[Even] the high priest and the whole council of elders can testify about me" (Acts 22:5).

The term's meaning expands when Paul invokes God as witness to acts of his interior life: "For God … is my witness that without ceasing I remember you always in my prayers" (Rom 1:9). The verb *marturein* refers to giving testimony to facts that have been seen and experienced (Acts 22:5); likewise, to bring a favorable testimony of good reputation (Acts 6:3). One can also invoke the testimony of God, the Spirit, and scripture: "All the prophets testify about him that everyone who believes in him receives forgiveness of sins through his name" (Acts 10:43). This last usage links testimony with the center of the Christian faith and gives to it the almost technical meaning of confessing or professing the faith.

St. Luke

According to St. Luke, the *martus* is at the same time a witness to the facts of the life of Jesus and to their meaning for the faith and its proclamation. "He said to them, 'Thus it is written, that the Messiah is to suffer and to rise from the dead on the third day, and that repentance and forgiveness of sins is to be proclaimed in his name to all nations, beginning from Jerusalem. You are witnesses of these things'" (Lk 24:46–48). In Paul's speech to the Jews at Pisidia: "But God raised him from the dead; and for many days he appeared to those who came up with him from Galilee to Jerusalem, and they are now his witnesses to the people. And we bring you the good news" (Acts 13:30–32). In the text, the appropriation of the title *martus* is reserved for the apostles, who were the eyewitnesses of the life and appearances of Jesus. The title is not applied to Paul or to Barnabas.

Nevertheless, one notes in Acts a certain distancing with respect to the meaning [of martyr as] witnessing of events from Jesus' life. Paul is called to be a witness for Jesus before all humanity on the basis of what he saw and heard—namely, the vision of Jesus on the road to Damascus (Acts 22:14–15, 26:16). Paul calls the deacon Stephen a witness to Jesus (Acts 22:20). Paul speaks of "the blood of your witness Stephen." Note here that the deacon Stephen is not called *martus* because he died for Jesus, but rather that he dies because of his witness to Christ in his evangelical activity. We therefore do not yet have the technical Christian sense of martyrdom attached to death, but it is nevertheless a preparation.

St. John

Although it is sometimes used in the common sense—for example, when John the Baptist says to the Jews, "You yourselves are my witnesses that I said, 'I am not the Messiah, but I have been sent ahead of him'" (1 Jn 3:28)—the terms *marturein*, to testify, and *marturia*, testimony (John uses neither *martus* nor *marturion*) have in the Johannine corpus the specific meaning of testimony on behalf of Jesus. This testimony does not bear directly upon Jesus' historical reality, though it is presupposed, nor on the events of his historical life—his birth, Passion, and Resurrection[1]—but rather it addresses, by means of this history and these events, the nature and meaning of his person, with the aim of eliciting faith in Jesus.

Such was the testimony of John the Baptist: "He came as a witness to give testimony to the light, so that all might believe in him" (1 Jn 1:7). John testifies that "the Word was the true Light" (1 Jn 1:8). His testimony concerns the eternity of Jesus: "John bore witness to him. He proclaimed, "Here is the one of whom I said: he who comes after me ranks ahead of me, because he was before me" (1 Jn 1:15). He also testifies to his capacity as the Son of God: "Yes, I have seen and have attested that this is the Son of God (or the Chosen One of God)" (1 Jn 1:34).

However, John's testimony on behalf of Jesus is exceeded by that of the Father: "But I have a testimony greater than John's. The works that the Father has given me to complete, the very works that I am doing, testify on my behalf that the Father has sent me. And the Father who sent me has himself testified on my behalf" (1 Jn 5:36–37). In this way, the Father's testimony combines with that of Jesus himself: "In your law it is written that the testimony of two witnesses is valid. I testify on my own behalf, and the Father who sent me testifies on my behalf" (1 Jn 8:17–18).

This testimony focuses on Jesus' identity as the Son of God in the strongest, most divine sense. This identity is already indicated insofar as Jesus refers to God "the Father," as "my Father." It is on account of such a claim that the Jews sought to stone him: "'you, though only a human being, are making yourself God.' Jesus answered them: 'you say that [I am] blaspheming because I said, "I

1. The one exception being the thrust of the lance in 1 Jn 19:35.

am God's Son" ... know and understand that the Father is in me and I am in the Father'" (1 Jn 10:30–38).

What is more, we could say that the entire Gospel of John is a collection of testimonies revealing the person of Jesus: [Jesus is revealed] to Nicodemus as the only Son sent by the Father to save all those who believe in him (1 Jn 3:16); to the Samaritan woman as the Christ (1 Jn 4:25–26); and to the Samaritan townspeople as the Savior of the world (1Jn 4:42); likewise, as the Bread and Wine (1 Jn 6:48), and as the Good Shepherd (1 Jn 10:11). These diverse attributions always conclude to Jesus' filial relation with the Father.

The drama of Jesus is tied up precisely in this testimony that he is the Son of God: the darkness has not understood the light, and his own did not receive him in his glory as the Father's only Son (1 Jn 1:11, 14). "Those who believe in the Son of God have the testimony in their hearts. Those who do not believe in God have made him a liar by not believing in the testimony that God has given concerning his Son" (1 Jn 5:10).

Through faith, the testimony of God penetrates into those who believe: "this is the testimony of God that he has testified to his Son. Those who believe in the Son of God have the testimony in their hearts" (1 Jn 5:9–10).

After Jesus' departure, the testimony is given by the Holy Spirit: "When the Advocate comes, whom I will send to you from the Father, the Spirit of truth who comes from the Father, he will testify on my behalf. You also are to testify because you have been with me from the beginning" (1 Jn 15:26–27). The testimony of the Spirit takes place through baptism (water) and the Eucharist (blood) (1 Jn 5:5–11).

The disciples too testify through their confession on behalf of Jesus: "You also are to testify because you have been with me from the beginning" (1 Jn 15:27). "And we have seen and do testify that the Father has sent his Son as the Saviour of the world" (1 Jn 4:14).

For St. John, the testimony always involves a historical reference, but the accent is markedly different from St. Luke. It takes on a deeper meaning: it proceeds from the knowledge of Jesus, from his glory as the Father's only Son, manifested through the Spirit. This glory is revealed to believers, making them sons of God according to a new birth. From then on, through faith, new witnesses to Jesus, distinct from the apostles, can arise, for the testimony of Jesus is in them: "Those who believe in the Son of God have the testimony in their hearts" (1 Jn 5:10).

In John's Apocalypse, the term *martus* is associated with the death of the faithful one on account of Jesus. The angel says to the church at Pergamon, "you are holding fast to my name, and you did not deny your faith in me even in the days of Antipas my witness, my faithful one, who was killed among you, where Satan lives" (1 Jn 2:13). And further on: "I saw that the woman was drunk with the blood of the saints and the blood of the witnesses to Jesus" (1 Jn 17:6). These uses of *martus* are quite close to the technical sense of martyrdom.

In Revelation and in Acts (in the case of the deacon Stephen), the Christian conception of martyrdom as death for Christ is anticipated—sketched [, as it were]. The specific definition of Christian martyrdom will soon establish itself in the early church through the convergence of the [then] current meaning of the word *martus* with the primitive Christian notion of active testimony on behalf of the truth of the Gospel, by the most perfect and definitive testimony—that is, that given under threat and torture until death.

The Testimony of Christ

We must pay special attention to some texts that accord to Christ the title *martus* or that speak of his [own] testimony, since they reveal to us, beyond the [mere] words themselves, the primary source of the testimony that defines Christian martyrdom.

In Revelation, Jesus is twice described as "the faithful witness" (Rv 1:5 and 3:17), however without mention of the Passion: "And to the angel of the church in Laodicea write: The words of the Amen, the faithful and true witness" (Rv 3:14). Note that the author of the Acts of the Martyrs of Lyon wrote, "If any of us, either in writing or in speech, addressed them by this title, they sharply reproved them, for they gladly yielded the salutation of 'witness' to Christ, the Faithful and True Witness and First-begotten of the dead, and God's Prince of Life."[2]

St. Paul writes to Timothy, "In the presence of God, who gives life to all things, and of Christ Jesus, who in his testimony before Pontius Pilate made the good confession, I charge you" (1 Tm 6:13). And further on: "Christ Jesus, himself human, who gave himself a ransom for all—such is the testimony (*marturion*) [which was] given at the right time.[3] For this I was appointed a herald and an apostle" (1 Tm 2:6).

These texts indicate to us the model of the apostles' elemental testimony (and later that of Christians and martyrs): the testimony given by Jesus at his trial before the Great Priest and before [Pontius] Pilate. We are also led to texts in which the history and drama of Jesus are concentrated, texts that constitute the decisive point of his Passion. It is on account of this testimony that Jesus will be condemned to death

The testimony of Jesus during his Passion bears precisely upon his very person: it is the solemn revelation of his identity as the

2. Tertullian, *Epistle of the Gallican Churches Lugdunum and Vienna*, trans. T. Herbert Bindley (New York: E. and J. B. Young, 1900), 45.

3. The passage "such is the testimony (*marturion*) [that was] given" is Pinckaers' own rendering of this passage. We have kept it as such in order to preserve the point he wishes to draw from it. The brackets themselves were also in the original French text [Tr.].

Son of God before the Jews and of his royalty before Pilate. "Then the high priest said to him, 'I put you under oath before the living God, tell us if you are the Messiah, the Son of God.' Jesus said to him, 'You have said so. But I tell you, from now on you will see the Son of Man seated at the right hand of Power and coming on the clouds of heaven.' Then the high priest tore his clothes and said, 'He has blasphemed! Why do we still need witnesses? ... What is your verdict?' They answered, 'He deserves death'" (Mt 26:63–66; Mk 14:60ff; Lk 22:66ff). The testimony of Jesus concerning his status as Son of God is supported with a citation from Daniel that characterizes him as divine, which was [*sic*] the decisive grounds of his condemnation. This exchange reveals the most essential aspect of Christian testimony: the person of Jesus.

The testimony before Pilate (Lk; 1 Jn 18:33ff) focuses specifically upon the royalty of Jesus, his status as King of the Jews in accordance with the accusation brought against him. It discloses a more external aspect of his identity in a language that Pilate can understand. It bears mentioning that each of these two testimonies points out Jesus' silence, which receives notice by both the High Priest and Pilate, emphasizing the importance of the moment: "Jesus was silent" (Mt 26:63, 27:14).

We can thus link the Johannine texts to Jesus bearing witness to himself and thereby proclaiming himself as the one sent from the Father and as the Son of God. For John, the affirmation that Jesus is the Son of God sums up the whole of the Gospel, like a collection of related signs given "so that you may come to believe that Jesus is the Messiah, the Son of God, and that through believing you may have life in his name" (1 Jn 21:31). Similarly, the evangelist will sum up the Christian faith with these words: "who is it that conquers the world but the one who believes that Jesus is the Son of God?" (1 Jn 5:5). One may gather the entire Gospel in this single testimony: Jesus is truly the Son of God; for this reason he was put to death, but God has raised him from the dead and has given him the power to communicate life to all who believe.

When one begins with the testimony that Jesus gives about himself during his Passion, one can easily discern the path that leads to the Christian martyrs of the first centuries and understand why their testimony is linked so closely with their death. Jesus' affirmation of his personal identity as the Son of God is the primary and unique testimony that the testimony of every apostle and disciple will imitate. Just as the testimony of Jesus before the High Priest sends him to his death, the testimony of the apostles and early Christians would similarly elicit persecution and threats of death. It is upon a condemnation similar to that of Jesus that their testimony comes to its completion; that they fully become witnesses—*martyrs*. The link is already very clearly indicated in the missionary discourse of St. Matthew, which can only be understood in the context of the persecution that his Christian readers were already undergoing.

One can then better understand why early Christians so commonly thought of martyrdom as a reproduction of the Passion of Jesus, so much so that they brought out so prominently in their martyrologies all the detailed similarities between the death [of the martyr] and that of Christ: the essential core of martyrdom is the proclamation of faith in Jesus as the Son of God—that is, the Christian's adoption of Jesus' own testimony about himself. Hence the account of Stephen's martyrdom in Acts contains several features that resemble the narrative of the Passion: the accusation by false witnesses of having spoken against the Temple (Acts 7:13), the vision of heaven opening and the Son of Man standing at the right hand of God (Acts 7:56), the last words: Lord Jesus, receive my spirit (Acts 7:59), and the prayer to God that the sin of those who stone him not be held against them (Acts7:60). The passion of Polycarp of Smyrna is [written] from the same perspective:

"all the preceding events happened in order that the Lord might show us once again a martyrdom which is in accord with the gospel."[4]

In Subsequent Christian Vocabulary

It is in the church of Smyrna and in Asia Minor that we find, in the middle of the second century, the technical Christian sense of the term *martus* and its derivatives: in the *Acts of Polycarp* (19.1)—that is, in the homeland of the Apocalypse, which discloses the first clues as to its meaning: "Such was the account of blessed Polycarp who was, with the brothers from Philadelphia, the twelfth to suffer *martyrdom* at Smyrna; yet we remember him alone above the others, so that everywhere even the pagans speak of him. He was not only a famous teacher, but also an eminent *martyr*, whose *martyrdom*, conformed to the Gospel of Christ, all desire to imitate." We have no other evidence of this particular usage of the word *martyr* elsewhere at that time.

Henceforth the Christian vocabulary will apply the term *martyr* to those who have given testimony to Christ and to faith to the point of death and will reserve it for them alone. We will now properly call martyrs only those who have actually suffered death for Christ, in contrast to the designation "confessor," [which refers to those] Christians who have confessed their faith before judges, even under torture, but who have survived.

The difference between the titles of confessor and martyr is clearly expressed in the *Letter of the Churches of Vienne and Lyon* in 177. The Christians of whom this document speaks, already having given their testimony many times amid great torment, remark that "these are indeed 'witnesses' [*martyrs*], whom Christ has deemed worthy to be taken up in their confession, since He

4. "Martyrdom of Polycarp," in *Apostolic Fathers*, 135.

sealed their witness by their death, [the seal of martyrdom]; but we are merely humble *confessors*."[5]

Later, however, the application of the term *martyr* would progressively extend to include not only those Christians who died for the faith amid torture, but also those who died in prison or in exile, and sometimes even to exiles who had returned to their homeland. The new step will then be establishing not equality, since the shedding of blood confers an incomparable dignity, but a certain assimilation of the martyr and the virtuous man who lacked the opportunity to suffer for the faith and whose own proper title is now that of confessor.

At the beginning of the fifth century, St. Augustine, sensing that the term *martyr* was no longer understood in its original sense by his Latin audience, reminds them in his first sermon on the First Letter of St. John how "some of the brethren who are not acquainted with the Greek do not know what the word 'witnesses' is in Greek: and yet it is a term much used by all, and held in religious reverence; for what in our tongue we call 'witnesses' [*testes*] in Greek are 'martyrs' [*martyres*]. Now where is the man that has not heard of martyrs, or where the Christian in whose mouth the name of martyrs dwells not every day? ... Well then, [to say] 'We have seen and are witnesses,' is as much as to say, 'We have seen and are martyrs. For it was for bearing witness of that which they had seen, and bearing witness of that which they had heard from them who had seen, that, while their testimony itself displeased the men against whom it was delivered, the martyrs suffered all that they did suffer. The martyrs are God's witnesses. It pleased God to have men for His witnesses, that men also may have God to be their witness."[6]

5. Tertullian, *Epistle of the Gallican Churches*, 45; emphasis added.

6. "Homily I on the Epistle of John to the Parthians (1 Jn 1:1–2:11)," in *Nicene and Post-Nicene Fathers*, translated by H. Browne, edited by Philip Schaff, 7:787, 1st

Isidore of Seville, for his part, writes [that] "we call them 'martyrs' in Greek and 'witnesses' in Latin, because they are suffering or have suffered on behalf of [their] testimony to Christ, and because they have fought to the death for truth."[7]

Conclusion

The evolution of the sense of *martus* in the Christian vocabulary clearly reveals to us the primary and central element of martyrdom and its spirituality. The concept that first confronts us and that we find throughout this evolution is that of testimony. However, this testimony becomes precise and more profound in the language of the New Testament in the following way:

1. Testimony in favor of the facts, events, and words of Jesus. This sense is especially appropriate to the apostles;
2. Testimony bearing upon the meaning of these events and words, and upon their universal salvific significance for the faith;
3. Testimony bearing upon the person of Jesus, on his status as the Son of God, sent from the Father, revealed to faith and rejected by the Jews. This is the Johannine sense of the term;
4. Testimony given to Christ to the point of death. This sense of the term appears in the Apocalypse.

These different meanings are interrelated and allow us to penetrate into the reality of Christian martyrdom: the testimony in favor of the principal events and words of the life of Jesus is relevant to their fuller meaning, which consists in the mystery of the person of Jesus and his divinity; this testimony is given unto death as a reproduction of the Passion of Jesus and as a supreme seal of authenticity.

---

series (Grand Rapids, Mich.: Christian Classics Ethereal Library); available online at http://www.ccel.org/ccel/schaff/npnf107.pdf; accessed May 2014.

7. St. Thomas cites this text in book IV of the *Sentences*, dist. 49, art.3, q.2, obj.9.

We might describe this conception of martyrdom as a performative summary of the gospel. St. John expressed its apex, its spiritual summit: it is bearing witness to the person of Jesus, to what is revealed by him through faith, [and] to the reality of the Resurrection and the new life that it makes possible. The truth of this interior revelation corresponds to its exterior manifestation: in the events of the life, Passion, and Resurrection of Jesus, and then [in turn] in the passion and courageous death of the martyrs, who were enlightened by the power of the Spirit.

The Object of the Martyrs' Testimony

If the martyr is above all a witness, an important question arises that has been widely discussed by historians: what exactly is the object with which this testimony concerns itself? Taken in itself, testimony has for its object events that have been closely observed, in person or through an intermediary. One such testimony could be provided by the apostles, who knew Jesus closely and witnessed his death, and then the appearances of the risen Christ. Things are already somewhat different for St. Paul, who never lived with Jesus. But the situation is entirely different for the martyrs who came after him, living more than a century after the actual events. How could we possibly refer to them as martyrs in the original sense of being witnesses?

The Leading Responses

Here are the leading responses to this question as presented by Fr. Delehaye:[8]

1. According to M. Geffcken, the Christian notion of martyrdom came from Stoicism, particularly from Epictetus. It consists

8. See Delehaye, "Sanctus," in *Les légendes hagiographiques* (Brussels: Société des Bollandistes, 1927), 95–108.

in the testimony on behalf of God through the practices of teaching and living a virtuous life, even at the price of well-being and liberty. And so according to Epictetus, the "martyr" or witness is a sage, a model who demonstrates that the doctrine taught by the Stoics is able to be practiced, as can be a life that is natural, humble, and lived in the open air. One may counter this hypothesis by replying that besides the word *martus*, one searches in vain in these texts for any characteristics reminiscent of Christian martyrdom.

2. According to Saint Matthew, the martyr is a witness speaking under the action of the Spirit: "When they hand you over, do not worry about how you are to speak or what you are to say; for what you are to say will be given to you at that time; for it is not you who speak, but the Spirit of your Father speaking through you" ([Mt] 10:19–20). The martyr is a witness to things to which others are not in a position to attest; he is supposedly endowed with a prophetic charism (Kattenbusch). However, neither the martyrs nor the confessors were ever described as prophets.

3. Martyrdom is an attestation of what others have not seen, such as the testimony of a vision of Jesus and the supernatural realm granted to the martyrs in the moments leading up to their death, in the same way that Stephen saw Christ at the right hand of God in the Acts of the Apostles ([Acts] 7:56). Or again, martyrs, like the apostles, are witnesses to the risen Christ through the special grace which they have been given to see the Lord and the supernatural realm at the moment of their death (K. Holl).

Yet the vision of Stephen seems to be an exceptional case. Moreover, the Acts of the Martyrs do not substantiate this explanation.

4. The martyr attests to the purity, holiness, and truth of a maligned doctrine, and reinforces its affirmation through the sacrifice of his life.

To this definition Fr. Delehaye objects that the Acts of the Martyrs do not make mention of any doctrinal declarations; the accusation simply concerns membership in a proscribed religion.

5. The *Letter of the Churches of Vienne and Lyon* reserve the title of martyr to Christ himself and to those whom he deigned to receive in confession after having imprinted on them, in death, the seal of martyrdom. St. Ignatius depicts his desire for martyrdom as an aspiration to become an imitator and disciple of Christ in his passion. [For him], only death is able to make him a perfect disciple. Hence martyrdom would be essentially a participation in Christ's title as the martyr *par excellence*, through the imitation of his Passion.

The difficulty here is the establishment of an equivalence between the notions of martyr and imitator, of witness (*martus*) and image (*eikôn*).

6. Fr. Delehaye, for his part, eventually concludes that it is a false problem and that the word *martyr* has simply changed its meaning in the Christian language: it not only signifies a witness, but one who imitates Christ to the point of death. In this way he eliminates the problem to which he sees no solution, by relegating it to the philological realm.

Our Response

We will not be as restrictive as Fr. Delehaye. By restricting the problem solely to philology, he dismisses from his consideration the inherently spiritual content of Christian martyrdom, which, in all likelihood, has played a causal role in the evolution of the meaning of the word *martyr*. If the responses to the question on the essence of the testimony of martyrdom are insufficient, it is doubtless because they fail to express the richness of the lived experience of the early Christians or else because they refuse to envision the martyrs from their [own] perspective of faith, which was all-determining. It is precisely this richness that interests us most and that we shall try to draw out from the testimony of the martyrs themselves, as the authentic Acts relate. Maybe then we can better understand in what way the testimony given on behalf of Christ influenced the philological evolution of the term *martyr* in Greek.

Let us take up the question again: what is the fact about which the martyrs give their testimony, so that they can properly be witnesses?

Seen against the horizon of their faith, it is of course the events of the life, death, and Resurrection of Jesus. [It also includes] his teachings, which bring to light the meaning [of these events], as well as the preaching of the apostles, who were the first and immediate witnesses [of these events]. Yet these teachings, together with the events of which they speak, would be too distant in time to properly attribute the title *witness* to anyone who would receive it later, unless something occurred in his life that actualized and verified in his own experience these ancient testimonies: we will refer to this as "the Jesus fact or event." It is conveyed in the simple phrase "I am a Christian" from the Acts of the Martyrs, which means for them, "I belong to Christ; Christ is here, alive, he is with us, he acts in us, he gives us his power, we are his, and he introduces us now into a new life."

In this Jesus event, we shall discern a twofold aspect: one interior and primary and the other exterior and secondary.

The Internal Aspect of the Jesus Event

1. The object of the martyrs' witness is the penetration of Christ's presence in them. That presence first changed the meaning of their life and conduct through faith; but it became particularly active and apparent at the moment when they were called to

testify on his behalf and to fight the decisive battle for him in the face of death. At that moment, the martyrs possessed an unwavering conviction that Christ had clothed them with his strength amid every fear and torment and that it was Christ himself who was acting, fighting, suffering, and prevailing in them.

Let us cite Ignatius of Antioch to the Church at Smyrna (IV.2): "'near the sword' means 'near to God'; 'with the beasts' means 'with God.' Only let it be in the name of Jesus Christ.... I endure everything because he himself, who is perfect man, empowers me."[9]

The martyrs of Lyon recount young Blandina: "For while we were all afraid for her ... ; Blandina was filled with such power that she was set free from and contrasted with those who tortured her.... But the blessed woman, like a noble athlete, gained her strength by her confession.... For she, small and weak and despised as she was, put on Christ, the great and resistless Athlete, and having worsted the adversary in many contests, won through conflicts the wreath of incorruption."[10]

In the Acts of the Martyrs of Smyrna: "Seeing them, we all understood that at the moment when they were being tortured, the martyrs of Christ were raptured out of their bodies, or rather that the Lord was present with them" (II.2).

In the *Martyrdom of Perpetua and Felicity*, Felicity, in the pains of childbirth, replies: "What I am suffering now ... I suffer by myself. But then another will be inside me who will suffer for me, just as I shall be suffering for him."[11]

The testimony of the martyrs is thus internally linked to that of Christ himself in his Passion. It is Christ in them, the unique

9. "St. Ignatius, Letter to the Smyrnaeans," in *Apostolic Fathers*, 111.

10. Tertullian, *Epistle of the Gallican Churches*, 29, 37–38.

11. "The Martyrdom of Perpetua and Felicity," in *The Acts of the Christian Martyrs*, edited and translated by Herbert Musurillo (New York: Oxford University Press, 1972).

Witness and the true martyr, who repeats his testimony, more so through actions than through words.

2. For the martyrs, the Jesus event is not simply a religious conviction or a subjective experience. It is an experience of reality capable of withstanding torture. It originates from Christ's active presence among them, from his conversation with them, as one person is revealed to another. This is an illuminating event, acquainting them with the mystery of Christ as the Son of God, and causing them, as it were, to take leave of themselves to the point where they become insensible to pain.

The martyrs of Lyon recall how Blandina "was repeatedly launched into the air by the beast [a bull].... Yet on account of her hope and firm hold on the things entrusted to her and her dialogue with Christ ... [she was] no longer sensible of her sufferings." Similarly, Alexander, facing the beasts, "neither murmured nor groaned at all, but [simply] conversed with God in his heart."[12]

The martyrs of Smyrna "also saw, with the eyes of the soul, the good things reserved for those who suffer, those good things which neither ear has heard, nor eye has seen, nor the human mind has conceived. The Lord showed them those good things."

Hence in a concrete way, without needing an explicit doctrinal statement, the testimony of the martyrs agrees with the testimony of the Gospel in its essential content, in its central teaching that Jesus is the Christ and the Son of God. By means of the simple affirmation "I am a Christian!" the testimony of the martyrs resumes in a personal mode the message of the evangelists and there links up with it.

At the same time, the testimony of the martyrs manifests an ecclesial and communal dimension. It is inscribed in the church's testimony to Christ based on the Gospels. It is important to note

12. Tertullian *Epistle of the Gallican Churches, Martyrdom of Perpetua*, 29, 41–42.

that the most authentic Acts are letters of the ecclesial communities, whether Smyrna or Lyon, and clearly demonstrate the communal scope of the testimonies, which were rendered in mutual support and fraternal example.

We are therefore dealing with an event at once both personal and ecclesial, occurring directly at the level of one's life of faith in Jesus. For this reason, while addressing the outside world, this event can only be truly transmitted through a testimony that awakens faith and thereby leads one into the realities of which it speaks.

3. The testimony of the martyrs focuses on the Passion and Resurrection of Christ and more precisely on entry into eternal life with the risen Christ, insofar as [the martyrs'] suffering, death, and victory song reproduce and actualize the events of the Gospel with such authenticity that they feel that it is Christ himself who suffers in them and overcomes in them the Devil, their persecutors, and death itself. For them, the Passion and Resurrection of Jesus are no longer past events, but rather take on the most poignant actuality in the face of suffering and death: the martyrs testify that Christ opens to them the way of life at [exactly] the point where others only see torment and annihilation. To express the scope of this testimony, one might use the following reasoning: if Christ had not died and risen for us, if he were not truly the Son of God, then he would not be able to help his witnesses in such an actual and effective way, nor would he be able to communicate to them a superhuman power and a joy that is already triumphant even in the midst of their suffering.

Let us cite the Acts of the Martyrs of Lyon. Sanctus, completely dismembered, had outwardly lost all human form. Yet "in him Christ suffered and achieved great glory, bringing the adversary to naught, and showing that there is nothing fearful where the Father's love is nor painful where is Christ's glory."[13]

13. Ibid., 30.

The martyrs are therefore directly in line with the yearning for death so as to be with Christ that St. Paul expresses in his Letter to the Philippians: "to know Christ and the power of his resurrection and the sharing of his sufferings by becoming like him in his death, if somehow I may attain the resurrection from the dead" (Phil 3:8–11).

We hear a direct echo of this text in the *Letter of St. Ignatius to the Romans*: "It is better for me to die for Jesus Christ than to rule over the ends of the earth. Him I seek, who died on our behalf; him I long for, who rose again for our sake. The pains of birth are upon me.... Let me receive the pure light, for when I arrive there I will be a man. Allow me to be an imitator of the suffering of my God. If anyone has Him within himself, let him understand what I long for and sympathize with me, knowing what constrains me."[14]

With regard to the present reproduction of the Passion of Christ, the testimony of the martyrs merges with that of the apostles. Concerning the latter, it is fitting to observe that their testimony has a greater density than that of occasional witnesses to the external events of Jesus' life, as they might be related by a Jewish or Roman spectator who happened to come across them. Beyond the visible facts, the testimony [of the apostles] focuses first and foremost on the new realities that have made the Passion and Resurrection of Christ appear before their eyes and in their life. They were witnesses not only of external events, but of a new reality made possible by Christ and centered on him.

It is precisely this testimony that the martyrs perpetuate. Though they did not behold Christ historically with their physical eyes, they know him in the actuality of his Passion and Resurrection, which they relive in their own trial, accepted for his sake. In this way they are able to make the substance of the apostles'

14. "Letter of Ignatius to the Romans," in *Apostolic Fathers*, 104.

testimony their own. The martyrs are witnesses of an event both ancient and ever-present, whose reality and meaning agree with the very testimony of the apostles.

4. Although the testimony of the martyrs deals with an event of the interior life, in the order of faith, this fact manifests its reality in the most tangible way because [this event takes on] physical shape in the torments that they endure with a strength of soul so powerful that it astonishes even their executioners. "Blandina was filled with such power that she was set free from and contrasted with those who tortured her with every kind of torture in turn from morning to evening, and who confessed that they were conquered, since they had nothing left which they could any longer do to her."[15]

This is why Ignatius of Antioch, in opposition to the Docetists who denied the reality of the Incarnation and the suffering of Jesus, puts forth the argument of his own suffering to testify to the truth of the Lord's Passion: "For if these things were done by our Lord in appearance only, then I am in chains in appearance only. Why, moreover, have I surrendered myself to death, to fire, to sword, to beasts? But in any case, 'near the sword' means 'near to God'; 'with the beasts' means 'with God.' Only let it be in the name of Jesus Christ!"[16]

In this way the Jesus event becomes a fact that the pagans themselves may witness, but that is more a performative testimony, through the victory over suffering, than a verbal one. One might say that it is a "testimony event."

5. Martyrdom is essentially a testimony to Christ, to a new and greater reality that has penetrated into the lives of the martyrs and that, through them, deeply impacts the lives of fellow Christians and even pagans. That mediation, made possible by the passion of

15. Tertullian, *Epistle of the Gallican Churches*, 28.
16. "Letter of Ignatius to the Smyrnaeans," in *Apostolic Fathers*, 111.

the martyrs and their proclamation of Christian identity, is rightly considered to be a testimony. The power of that testimony comes from the fact that it engages the entire being, words and actions, body and soul, life and death, and that it reveals the intervention of a power greater than man. Indeed, the most fundamental element of Christian martyrdom is the action of Christ in those who suffer for him: that which must be recognized and explained in order to understand and explain their actions. All the elements that enter into martyrdom—doctrine, conviction, courage, signs and visions, tortures—must order themselves around this primary element: Christ, as the object of testimony, of faith, and of love.

The External Aspect of the Jesus Event

The Jesus event, which serves as the basis of the martyrs' testimony, also has an external dimension, as does this testimony, whether before the Roman authority who judges and condemns or before the pagans who witness a martyrdom.

1. At first glance one can already say that the martyrs merit the title of witnesses solely from the fact that they must appear before the Roman tribunals just as Jesus did. They doubtless appear as the accused in the eyes of their judges, but in their own eyes they are judged not in their own name, but on account of Christ's. They therefore consider themselves to be witnesses on Christ's behalf before these tribunals, and the church also regards them as such. This simple affirmation continually returns to the mouths of the martyrs when they are interrogated, summing up their testimony: "I am a Christian!"

2. When one probes the content of this testimony before the pagans, the first thing that appears is the affirmation of one and only one God and Creator, in opposition to the false gods to which the Roman religion and the imperial authorities want them to offer sacrifice. The bishop Cyprian remarks, "I am a Christian

and a Bishop. I do not recognize any god other than the one true God, who has made the heaven and the earth, the sea and all that it contains. It is this God that we serve day and night, for our own sake and for the sake of all humanity, and even for the sake of the emperors' salvation."

Such an affirmation is directly occasioned by the accusation that Christians were atheists or adversaries of the gods. It is not surprising [then] that Christ is not mentioned under the titles assigned to him in scripture, anymore than they appear in St. Paul's speech at Athens.

3. However, when Christ himself is attacked, the preferred response is one that appeals to his title as King, in opposition to the imperial power and its absolutist pretentions. Take Polycarp, for example: "when the magistrate persisted and said, 'Swear the oath, and I will release you; revile Christ,' Polycarp replied, 'for eighty-six years I have been his servant, and he has done me no wrong. How can I blaspheme my King who saved me?' But he continued to insist, saying 'You who swear by the genius of Caesar and pretend not to know who I am, listen carefully: I am a Christian.'"[17]

This text communicates to us the content of the term *Christian*: "I belong to Christ as to my King and my Savior; I therefore do not belong to Caesar." [At the same time] Polycarp immediately makes it clear that Christians are taught to give proper respect to the authorities and powers established by God. This text obviously recalls St. John's version of Jesus' appearance before Pilate, when Jesus claims the title of King in the world of the truth to which he bears witness, and then assures [Pilate] that he has no power over him that is not given to him from on high (1 Jn 18:37–19:11).

One could say, then, that martyrdom is the testimony of a dis-

17. "Martyrdom of Polycarp," in *Apostolic Fathers*, 139.

ciple's allegiance to Christ as King, which prohibits obedience to any human authority, even the supreme authority, if it orders an act disowning [that allegiance]. Thus the external dimension of martyrdom, just like the internal dimension, is ordered to the Passion of Jesus.

The proceedings of the conscription of Maximilian, who refused to be a soldier because he was a Christian, express in a particularly nice way the consciousness of the incompatibility between belonging to Christ and worldly allegiances. "I will not be a soldier. Let me be beheaded. I do not serve the world; I serve my God.... I do not accept the *signaculum* [seal] of the world. If one attaches it to me, I will break it, for it is worthless. I am a Christian, and so I am not permitted to wear lead upon my neck, on top of the saving *signaculum* of my Lord Jesus Christ, son of the living God."[18]

Conclusion

Christian martyrdom, as it appears in the authentic documents, contains enough of the essential components of testimony that the idea was able to survive the whole length of the evolution of the Greek term *martus* up to the development of its Christian sense of testimony unto death in imitation of the Passion of Christ. It is clearly a testimony of a particular kind, since it concerns a new reality that exceeds the experience of those who lack faith. Yet it is precisely for this reason that the testimony is especially necessary, both in word and deed, in order that the reality of which it speaks may be communicated. Martyrdom is therefore one of the forms—indeed, the most complete form—of testimony linked to the transmission of the faith: [a testimony] to the spiritual realities that that faith reveals to us.

Christianity has found in the classical term *martus* a word

18. Paul Monceaux, *La vrai légende dorée,* 252–53.

particularly well suited to the proper mode of communicating the realities of the faith; but in utilizing it, Christians have inserted it into a context of new and greater life. This usage has inevitably brought about an evolution and a refinement of this word: testimony through suffering and death on behalf of the risen Christ. That sense of the word became so prominent that its root passed unmodified into other languages whose literal translation of the word (*testis* in Latin, *temoin* in French, *witness* in English) often bore no philological correspondence with it, thus leading to a loss of the primary and specific meaning of Christian martyrdom.

ADDITIONAL NOTES

Note 1: The Juridical Basis of Christian Persecution

There has been much discussion about the juridical basis of Christian persecution.[19] On this topic, we should note the general tolerance of the Romans with respect to the cults of foreign nations. That tolerance extended, among others, to the Jews, who because of their monotheism, denied the gods of Greece and Rome, but who were nevertheless granted the right to exercise their religion and their cult and were exempt from pagan ceremonies and even from military service. Christians, who were soon distinguished from the Jews and who were spread throughout all the pagan nations, were no longer able to claim this privilege and so were obliged to comply with the Roman legislation concerning the worship to be offered to their gods and emperors. Under Domitian the high priest came from Jerusalem to Rome to explain the difference between Jews and Christians so as to avoid confusion.

19. Leclercq, "Droit persécuteur," *DAL* 4 (1921), cols. 1565–1648; Daniel-Rops, *l'Église des âpotres et des martyrs* (Paris: Fayard, 1948), 185–86; J. Morlau, *Les persécutions du christianisme dans l'Empire romain* (Paris: Presses Universitaires de France, 1956).

With regard to the juridical basis for persecuting Christians, one can distinguish three fundamental systems underlying the various proposed solutions: the system of common law legislation, the system of coercion, and the system of ad hoc legislation banning Christianity as such, the latter being the most traditional explanation.

The System of Common Law Legislation

Christians would have been condemned under criminal charges, such as sacrilege or lese-majesté, on account of their refusal to sacrifice to the gods and to the emperor. Such accusations should be distinguished from the monstrous crimes attributed to Christians in the popular imagination, which could only be a basis for accusation after legal investigation.

[Yet] this explanation is inadequate, since the offenses of sacrilege and lese-majesté had a very precise definition in Roman law. [These crimes] presupposed a positive action: the theft of a sacred object in a temple or a desecration of an image of the emperor: in other words, a specific occurrence that had to be proven in order for a punishment to ensue. But when it came to Christians, the procedure was different. Instead of seeking to determine whether the individual brought before him had committed such and such an act, the magistrate simply confined himself to asking the question, "Are you a Christian?" Upon an affirmative response and persistence in that profession, he would pronounce the sentence. There is no question of establishing any facts about acts of sacrilege or lese-majesté. The designation *Christian* is the only matter of importance. Therefore the refusal to sacrifice to the gods and Caesar, or to swear by the divine genius of the emperor, was not considered to be a capital crime according to common law.

However, this refusal played a considerable role in the lawsuits brought against Christians. For the injunctions rendered by the magistrate to sacrifice, to swear a pagan oath, or to commit any other act directly contrary to Christianity—to curse Christ, for example, or to eat forbidden food—were an investigative tool that the judge used when dealing with Christians. The refusal to obey these orders of the magistrate, while not technically a crime, furnished sufficient proof of one's Christian faith, the mere profession of which constituted a legal offense newly introduced into the penal code of the empire.

Note that the entire political agenda of Augustus, which was continued by his successors, was built upon the premise of consolidating personal power by placing all political, military, legal, and religious power in the hands of the emperor so as to maintain, in the wake of numerous conquests, the unity of an empire now made up of disparate nations. This resulted in the restoration of the Roman religion and the creation of the imperial cult, which posed a direct challenge to Christianity.

Yet it is not until the year 250 CE that the refusal to sacrifice to the gods became a legal rationale for prosecuting Christians under the emperor Decius, who, anxious to reestablish the unity of the national religion, promulgated an edict ordering all citizens to honor the gods under penalty of death.

The System of Coercion

The jurist [Theodor] Mommsen has elaborated a theory [claiming that] the repression of Christianity was carried out primarily through police action or coercion. "Alongside regular penal justice, applied to crimes, should be placed police regulations, which the Romans called *jus coercitionis*." Emanating from the omnipotence of the state, [this power] was given to all magistrates who participated in the *imperium*. Armed with this authority, they could enact on their own any measure they deemed necessary or expedient for the maintenance of order and the safeguarding of the national character of the Roman religion. They could force (*coercere*) their subordinates to obey and impose on the recalcitrant such punishment as seemed suitable to them, so long as it comported with law and custom. In religious matters, coercion occurred any time the public order was threatened or when it came to bolstering the exclusively nationalist character of Roman religion.

Yet Henri Leclercq believes that "regardless of how attractive it is, this conception of the first battles between the Roman state and the Christian Church does not seem able to withstand careful and impartial examination of the facts. All the documents link the prosecution of Christians to the exercise of criminal jurisdiction, not coercion."[20]

This explanation also conflicts with the rescript of Trajan that remained in force during the second century and until the middle of the third century as the organic law governing trials against Christians. This rescript forbade magistrates from exercising their spontaneity; they were required to wait for accusations according to the standard procedure, as anonymous accusations were not permitted. "Do not search for Christians, but if they are accused and convicted, then punish them. Yet if anyone denies being a Christian and confirms it by praying to our gods, he should be pardoned."

The Crime of Christianity

The traditional explanation of Christian persecution traces its origin to an imperial decree dating back to Nero or Domitian that Tertullian calls the *Institutum neronianum*. The text is no longer extant, but if it existed it probably contained these terms of proscription: "*Non licet esse christianos*" [Being a Christian is forbidden]. This expression underlies many sayings of authors such as Tertullian: "What a harsh law you have written, which says to

20. Leclercq, "Droit persécuteur," cols. 1584–86.

us: you are forbidden to exist" (*non licet esse vos*). The apologists consistently reaffirm that Christians were accused merely of being Christians; that they were reproached only for bearing that name, and Tertullian repeatedly asserts that the sentence condemning them indicates no other crime than that. The magistrate would remind the accused of that concise decree, "*non licet esse christianos*," to which the accused would reply, if he were faithful, "*christianus sum*" (I am a Christian), and the case would be closed.[21] This explanation relies upon Trajan's rescript of 112 CE in response to a letter from Pliny the Younger. Pliny displayed a rigorous but exact interpretation of the legislation, which he used to condemn Christians *propter solum nomen*—solely on account of the name:

> I make it a sacred duty, my lord, to consult you with my scruples, for who can better guide or instruct me? I have never attended the trial or sentencing of any Christian. I therefore do not know the exact offenses for which they are prosecuted nor the extent to which they are punished. I am particularly hesitant about whether to make distinctions according to age. Should we impose the same punishment without distinguishing the younger from the older? Should we pardon those who repent, or is the renunciation of Christianity useless once it has been embraced? Is it *the name only* that we punish? Or are there crimes attached to that name?

The emperor approves and confirms the obligation to punish *nomen si flagitiis careat* (the name, even without misdeeds) and not merely the *flagitia nomini coherentia* (the misdeeds associated with the name).

This rescript of Trajan presupposes an existent law against Christians, dating back at least to Nero or Domitian, which interpretation he solidifies. According to Tertullian, "Under the reign of Augustus this name [Christian] has arisen, under Tiberius it

21. Ibid., col. 1619.

has shown its discipline, and under Nero it has met with condemnation. Yet only this institution of Nero has survived, while the others were destroyed" (*Ad Nationes* 1.I, c.VII).

And so, legally speaking, this very characteristic of *being* a Christian would seem to serve as the basis of the persecution of the first centuries. The historians still debate the existence of that anti-Christian law. Some think that the legal precedent was laid down by Trajan's rescript itself. [But] regardless of the historical debate surrounding its legal origins, the persecuted Christians understood the basis of the accusation against them to be the mere fact that they were Christians: "*Non licet esse christianos.*"

Of course, from the perspective of the people and of Roman society generally, there were many nonjuridical reasons that helped to fuel these persecutions. Christianity appeared as a new religion born into the Roman Empire, consciously committed to the divine mission of unifying all men in a single faith, and as a result, uprooting paganism throughout the entire world. On account of this mission and the means it had to employ for its realization, Christianity would come into direct conflict with the fundamental principles on which Roman society rested, with respect both to its social and its political outlook on religion. As monotheists, Christians denied the existence of the various civic gods, whom they saw as mere trinkets of vague superstition, including the gods who wielded the most power, the ones most recently enshrined in Olympus: namely, the deified emperors. The morality practiced by Christians, whatever their obedience to existing laws and their loyalty to the emperors might be, comprised, on many points, a critique or negation of the present social order. Hatred of the human race seemed to be the heart of their doctrine. So says Dom Leclercq.[22] We might add that upon reading these documents and debates, we also sense that behind this encounter between Christianity and the pagan world

22. Ibid., col. 1570.

lies a mysterious confrontation exceeding the explanatory accounts proposed by historians.

Conclusion

The question we have just been examining is not merely of legal importance. If it is true that the persecutions were based on legislation aiming directly at Christian identity, we should note the astonishing correspondence of such an edict with the specifically Christian witness of the martyrs, which focused upon belonging to Christ in both an interior and exterior fashion, as we have just discussed. Even for Roman magistrates, then, there is no doubt that, whatever other crimes the populace may have attributed to them, the martyrs of the early centuries suffered precisely on account of their identity as Christians.

Note 2: The Difference between a Confessor and a Martyr

The question is the following: if *martyr* means witness, why would Christians who have given witness in favor of Christ before tribunals and amid tortures, but who have escaped death for one reason or another, not merit the title of "martyr" but only that of "confessor," as the *Letter from the Churches of Vienne and Lyon* would have it: "Those are martyrs whom Christ has deigned to receive in confession, having imprinted upon them, through death, the seal of martyrdom. As for us, we are only humble confessors"? It seems that there is no difference between confessors and martyrs with respect to giving witness. The distinction rests only on the accidental fact that some die and others survive. Therefore, the act of giving witness would not specifically define martyrdom, since it cannot distinguish the martyr from the confessor.

In our opinion, this objection considers the facts from too external a point of view, as if we were dealing with any testimony for an ordinary cause under the threat of death. It does not take sufficient account of the interiority of the martyrs' witness, of the properly Christian perspective that has nonetheless been the engine of this very linguistic evolution.

The objection neglects these two points:

1. For Christians, witness to the faith takes several forms and is therefore an analogical [term]. It concerns the preaching of the faith, often with persecution, catechesis, public profession of faith, confession, and martyrdom itself. These diverse forms attain their perfection, however, in martyrdom as a witness unto death, which provides the definitive seal. The witness of the apostles themselves, according to the tradition, required the seal of martyrdom. [Thus] there can be an [essential] continuity between the diverse forms of witness, such as confessor and martyr, even with their specific variations.

2. The objection neglects above all the following:

   a. *On the subjective plane:* witness does not consist solely in the words expressing a subjective conviction, but above all in an action, in the acceptance of torture whose crowning is death. Death is not accidental to the act of witness; death is already present to it as a threat, as a foreseen conclusion, and completes it by actualizing that conclusion. The fact of death is not indifferent; it consummates and finalizes the witness to Christ.

   b. *On the objective plane:* the witness has its intentional and causal center in Christ's Passion, which it actively reproduces. From the Christian point of view, the witness is thereby complete only if the confessor has seen this imitation of the Passion through until the end, or rather if he has received the grace of the Passion in its fullness, brought to completion in death. The confessor is not a martyr: (1) because his witness has not received the seal of death that consummates and finalizes it, even from the human point of view; (2) because his witness is not yet complete as a reproduction of the Passion of Jesus, as reception of that grace which leads to participation in the Resurrection.

Note 3: Under What Conditions May a Christian Be Considered a Martyr?

We are tempted to answer this question by referring solely to the external dimension: when one is put to death on account of faith in Christ on account of the Christian religion. The difficulty is that the persecutor, who does not share this faith, will almost always have motives that are entirely unrelated to religion, which do not correspond to those of the Christian, and [thereby] obscure matters.

In order to be adequate, our response should be drawn from the internal dimension of martyrdom. What first makes the martyr is the action of Christ, reproducing in the believer his Passion, with its two dimensions of suffering until death and victory over death through the power of the Father's love. It is, at the same time, the acceptance by the Christian of suffering and death as a witness on behalf of Christ. Thus martyrdom entails an exterior dimension, insofar the witness is given in public before opponents threatening death.

In order for the martyrdom to be authentic, it is therefore not essential that the persecutor inflict death explicitly and uniquely because of belief in Christ, which nevertheless was clearly the case for the Christians of the first centuries. The most decisive component is [rather] the conscious and courageous affirmation by the Christian of the sovereignty and kingship of Christ in the face of a human imperialism that demands, under penalty of death, an action incompatible with the service of Christ and faith in him. One can be an authentic martyr for refusing to commit an injustice, for refusing to lie, for refusing to take an oath. However, the official recognition of a martyr by the church requires that the cause be clear, [and] that it be sufficiently established that the question of faith in Christ was directly involved.

The notion of martyrdom would later extend to Christian sanctity because of the similitude and kinship between [their] profound realities insofar as sanctity is the gift of one's entire life to Christ throughout trials and even unto the willing acceptance of actual death through faith in the Resurrection. Thus the monastic or consecrated life will be assimilated to martyrdom, not so much because of its difficulties but because of the gift unto death, *usque ad mortem*, which it entails for the sake of Christ.

3

MARTYRDOM AND THE EUCHARIST

The intimate link established in the first centuries between martyrdom and the Eucharist by St. Ignatius of Antioch, among others, is a fact very much worth our consideration.

1. THE LINK BETWEEN THE EUCHARIST AND THE PASSION

In order to understand the basis of the relationship between martyrdom and the Eucharist, one should recall the essential link established by the evangelists between the Eucharist and the Passion, of which martyrdom is a reproduction. In the Gospels, the Eucharist is an integral part of the Passion, as already indicated by the place of the institution narrative between the betrayal of Judas and Jesus' prediction of Peter's denial (Mt 26; Mk 14; Lk 22). St. Paul will concur: "Every time you eat this bread and drink this cup, you proclaim the death of the Lord until he comes again" (1 Cor 11:26).

The realism of the Eucharist corresponds to that of the Passion: Jesus suffered in his body and in his blood, which is to say in his soul, separated upon the cross. The Eucharist is the sacrament that expresses the Passion of Jesus in its corporeal reality and allows the disciples to communicate with [the Passion] as a food and a drink that nourish them in their own bodies and their spirits: "the reality, however, is the body of Christ" (Col 2:17).

The source of the Passion is the *agape* of the Father manifested in the sacrifice of Jesus: "The proof that God loves us is this: that while we were yet sinners, Christ died for us" (Rom 5:8), and its completion is Jesus' return to the Father through the resurrection. The Eucharist expresses the *agape* of Jesus through the gift of body and blood, material for a new worship that communicates under the species of food and drink the new life stemming from the Resurrection, sustaining in us the desire to follow Christ even in his suffering, so as one day to be reunited with him. "I will not drink the fruit of the vine again until the day when I will drink the new wine with you in the Kingdom of my Father" (Mt 26:29).

II. THE LINK BETWEEN THE EUCHARIST AND MARTYRDOM

We have seen that Christians understood martyrdom to be a reproduction of the Passion of Jesus. The link between the Passion and the Eucharist leads us then to establish a relation between the Eucharist and martyrdom.

1. The Eucharist appears first as the proper food for martyrdom, perfectly suited to sustain the courage of the martyrs amid the difficult battle that they wage on behalf of Christ and in imitation of him. Saint Ignatius writes, "I take no pleasure in corruptible food or the pleasures of this life. I want the bread of God, which is the flesh of Christ who is of the seed of David; and for drink I want his blood, which is incorruptible love."[1]

1. "Letter of Ignatius to the Smyrnaeans," in *Apostolic Fathers*, 105.

2. Martyrdom and the Eucharist [both] proceed from *agape*, from the love of Christ. The role of the Eucharist with respect to the martyrs is not limited merely to bolstering their courage. In this sacrament, the Christian receives the body and blood of Christ and becomes intimately united to him in *agape*, which is also the wellspring of martyrdom. In this Eucharistic *agape*, the Christian receives, under the veil of faith, the "Jesus event" and, as it were, Christ's [own] witness to himself, which the martyr's testimony before the judges then reproduces and echoes. Through the personal contact established in faith through the Eucharist, the light and strength of Christ pass into the Christian. This union extends itself into the greater unity of Christians gathered around the bishop in the celebration of a single Eucharist. "Let all of you run together as to one temple of God, as to one altar, to one Jesus Christ, who came forth from one Father and remained with the One and returned to the One."[2]

3. On the other hand, martyrdom brings about in the most realistic fashion that which the Eucharist signifies. [The Eucharist] nourishes in the Christian the seed of Jesus' *agape*. Through martyrdom, that seed reaches its full maturity in the gift that the Christian makes of his body and his blood by means of his suffering unto death. Martyrdom is therefore the realization of the Eucharist; it too proclaims, but through [the martyr's] actions, the death of Jesus until he comes again.

4. Let us note the realism of the Passion, the Eucharist, and martyrdom. We may rightly emphasize here St. Ignatius's special insistence, contra the Docetists, upon the real character of Christ's Passion and sufferings. We also find this realism in the Eucharist and in martyrdom. Just as Christ truly suffered in his body, so Ignatius suffers in his own body to the point of shedding blood, and

2. "Letter of Ignatius to the Magnesians," in *Apostolic Fathers*, 95.

it is also the body and blood of Jesus that Christians receive in the Eucharist, as fortifying nourishment. It is for this reason that the Docetists, denying the reality of the Passion, did not participate in the celebration of the Eucharist and rendered the sufferings of the martyrs pointless.

"He truly suffered just as he truly raised himself—not, as certain unbelievers say, that he suffered in appearance only.... For I know and believe that he is in the flesh even after the resurrection; and when he came to Peter and those with him, he said to them: 'Take hold of me; handle me and see that I am not a disembodied demon.' And immediately they touched him and believed, being closely united with his flesh and blood. For this reason they too despised death; indeed, they proved to be greater than death.... For if these things were done by our Lord in appearance only, then I am in chains in appearance only.... I endure everything because he himself, who is perfect man, empowers me."[3] "They abstain from the Eucharist and prayer, because they refuse to acknowledge that the Eucharist is the flesh of our Savior Jesus Christ, which suffered for our sins and which the Father by his goodness raised up."[4]

5. Martyrdom is also a sacrifice. Like the Passion and the Eucharist, martyrdom comes to be thought of as a sacrifice, an oblation of one's entire being to God: a cult, a liturgy. "Grant me nothing more than to be poured out as an offering to God while there is still an altar ready, so that in love [*agape*] you may form a chorus and sing to the Father in Jesus Christ, because God has judged the bishop from Syria worthy to be found in the West, having summoned him from the East. It is good to be setting from the world to God, in order that I may rise to him."[5] "I am God's

3. "Letter of Ignatius to the Smyrnaeans," 110–11.

4. Ibid., 112.

5. "Letter of Ignatius to the Romans," in *Apostolic Fathers*, 103.

wheat, and I am being ground by the teeth of the wild beasts, that I might prove to be pure bread."[6] We find the same perspective in the martyrdom of Polycarp: "May I be received among them in your presence today, as a rich and acceptable sacrifice, as you have prepared and revealed beforehand, and have now accomplished, you who are the undeceiving and true God."[7]

6. Martyrdom is inscribed into the unity of the body of Christ. Through the communion with Christ's body that it effects, the Eucharist realizes and reveals the union between the believers who make up the body of Christ, as 1 Corinthians 12:12 teaches.[8] The Jerusalem Bible observes that the basis for this teaching is Paul's faith in Jesus resurrected in his body through the Spirit, opening up a new world into which Christians are incorporated in their very bodies, through the rites of baptism and the Eucharist.

St. Ignatius, meanwhile, places particular emphasis upon the unity of Christians gathered around their bishop to celebrate a single Eucharist: "Take care, therefore, to participate in one Eucharist … for there is one flesh of our Lord Jesus Christ, and one cup which leads to unity through his blood; there is one altar, just as there is one bishop, together with the presbytery and the deacons."[9]

Martyrdom should be understood in the context of that unity of Christ's body and the church, particularly as that unity is signified by the one Eucharist. It is not simply an act of courage from the point of view of personal salvation; it has an ecclesial dimension. It helps to cement the unity of the church around Christ and issues through its testimony an invitation into the Body of Christ.

6. Ibid.

7. "The Martyrdom of Polycarp," in *Apostolic Fathers*, 141.

8. "For just as the body is one and has many members, and all the members of the body, though many, are one body, so it is with Christ."

9. "Letter of Ignatius to the Philadelphians," in *Apostolic Fathers*, 107.

7. The Eucharist nourishes, in a sacramental way, the hope of definitive union with Christ beyond death. The eschatological orientation of the Eucharist—proclaiming the death of Christ until he comes again—corresponds to the eschatological trajectory of martyrdom that is oriented, through death, to union with the risen Christ.

As an illustration, let us look at a homily of St. Augustine's given on the feast of St. Lawrence, an occasion on which he says it is not out of place to preach about the Eucharist, "about the body of the Lord which he promised to give us to eat that we might have eternal life." During his interrogation and torture, amid the fiery death inflicted upon him, Lawrence remained in the Lord. "In that slow death . . . , amidst those tortures, since he had eaten and drunk properly, fortified by that bread and inebriated by that cup, he was impervious to the tortures. He remained firmly united to the one who said *it is the Spirit that gives life*. Indeed his flesh would burn, but the Holy Spirit would give life to his soul. He did not give in, and so he entered into the Kingdom" (*Homily* 27 on Jn 1 and 12). St. Cyprian repeatedly voiced the same conviction in his correspondence: by drinking the cup of the Lord, men are able to find the strength to shed their blood for Christ. He writes, "A severer and a fiercer fight is now threatening, for which the soldiers of Christ ought to prepare themselves with uncorrupted faith and robust courage, considering that they drink the cup of Christ's blood daily, for the reason that they themselves also may be able to shed their blood for Christ."[10]

Thus in anticipation of a new wave of trials, the Council of Carthage in 253 CE decided to give absolution and communion to those who had apostatized during the persecution of Decius and

10. St. Cyprian, "Epistle 55," in *Ante-Nicene Fathers*, vol. 5; revised and edited for New Advent by Kevin Knight, http://www.newadvent.org/fathers/050655.htm; accessed May 2014.

were doing penance ever since.[11] [Referring to this decision, Augustine writes]: "the Eucharist should be a defense to those who receive it, and so those whom we desire to see defended against the adversary should be nourished and comforted by the Sunday meal. How can we teach them and invite them to spill their blood in the confession of Christ if we refuse them the blood of Christ when they go to fight? How can we render them capable of drinking the cup of martyrdom if we do not first allow them to drink the cup of the Lord in the church, on account of the regulations governing our communion?" (Augustine, *Letter* 57.2,2).

Augustine also applies to the martyrs the image of the "intoxicating cup" (Ps 22:5): "The martyrs were intoxicated by the cup when, going to torture, they no longer recognized their own. Is there a greater intoxication than that in which one no longer recognizes one's weeping spouse, children and parents? . . . Do not be astonished, for they were drunk. How did they become drunk? They received the intoxicating chalice" (on Ps 35:14).[12]

In tractate 47 on the Gospel of John, Augustine underlines another important aspect of the relation between the Eucharist and martyrdom—namely, that of the imitation of Christ the Good Shepherd who gives his life for his sheep. "He is not alone in having done so, and yet insofar as those who did do it are his members, he alone has done it, since he himself could do it without them, but as for them, how could they do it without him who said '*Without me you can do nothing*?'"

11. In the original French text, Pinckaers does not designate whether his dates are CE or BCE, presumably since the relevant sources and events he considers are without exception in the Common Era. In order to avoid all possible confusion, however, we have added "CE" to the end of all his dates [Tr.].

12. On Ps 35:14; see Marie-François Berrouard, in *Oeuvres de saint Augustin* (Paris: Études Augustinienne, 1988), v.72, note 74.

Conclusion

The close links that connect martyrdom to the Eucharist help to explain the association of the cult of the martyrs with the Eucharistic liturgy, which will eventually be extended by the bond between the cult of the saints and the Eucharist.

4

MARTYRDOM AND ESCHATOLOGY

I. THE ESCHATOLOGICAL PERSPECTIVE OF MARTYRDOM

The evangelists portray the Passion of Jesus, directed by the will of the Father expressed in the scriptures, as Jesus' passage from this world to his Father, leading to the Resurrection and his sitting at the Father's right hand until he returns again at the end of time. This is the account Jesus himself gives in his testimony before the Sanhedrin.

"From now on you will see the Son of Man seated at the right hand of Power and coming on the clouds of heaven" (Mt 26:64). "And if I go and prepare a place for you, I will come again and will take you to myself, so that where I am, there you may be also." (Jn 14:3). "I am going away, and I am coming to you.' If you loved me, you would rejoice that I am going to the Father ... but I do as the Father has commanded me, so that the world may know that I love the Father" (Jn 14:28–31).

The Eucharist, the sacrament of the Passion, likewise has an eschatological dimension: "I tell you, I will never again drink of this fruit of the vine until that day when I drink it new with you in my Father's kingdom" (Mt 26:29). "For as often as you eat this bread and drink the cup, you proclaim the death of the Lord until he comes again" (1 Cor 11:26).

Similarly, martyrdom came to be understood and lived out as a passage to the Father and to Christ who sits at his side. At the same time it includes, in a mysterious way, the manifestation of Christ to his witnesses, initially to support them and then ultimately to reveal and unite himself to them beyond the threshold of death. This phenomenon appears explicitly in the narrative of St. Stephen's martyrdom, which serves as the model for the first Christians: "And they saw that his face was like the face of an angel.... But filled with the Holy Spirit, he gazed into heaven and saw the glory of God and Jesus standing at the right hand of God. 'Look,' he said, 'I see the heavens opened and the Son of Man standing at the right hand of God!" (Acts 6:15 and 7:55–56).

We also find this perspective in St. Ignatius and in the martyrdom of Polycarp. "There is no more fire of material longing within me," writes Ignatius to the Romans, "but only water living and speaking in me: 'Come to the Father.'"[1] Polycarp prays as follows: "O Lord God Almighty ... I bless you because you have considered me worthy of this day and hour, that I might receive a place among the number of the martyred in the cup of your Christ, to the resurrection to eternal life, both of soul and of body, in the incorruptibility of the Holy Spirit."[2] The narrator of these Acts describes the martyrs this way: "Blessed and noble, therefore, are all the martyrdoms that have taken place in accordance with the will of God.... [They showed us] all that at the very hour when

1. "Letter of Ignatius to the Romans," in *Apostolic Fathers*, 105.
2. "The Martyrdom of Polycarp," in *Apostolic Fathers*, 141.

they were being tortured the martyrs of Christ were absent from the flesh, or rather that the Lord was standing by and conversing with them. And turning their thoughts to the grace of Christ they despised the tortures of this world, purchasing at the cost of one hour an exemption from eternal punishment. And the fire of their inhuman torturers felt cold to them, for ... with the eyes of their heart they gazed upon the Good things which are reserved for those who endure patiently, things 'which neither ear has heard nor eye has seen, nor has it entered into the heart of man,' but which were shown to them by the Lord."[3]

The spirituality of martyrdom thus assumes the eschatological dimension of the New Testament, but it influences our understanding of it by concentrating on the martyrs' passage to Christ amid their witness on his behalf, emphasizing the reception of the martyr in the Kingdom of eternal life. [This passage] can thus be conceived as synonymous with Christ's manifestation to those who suffer for him and in whom he suffers anew. Thus the Parousia, though situated at the end of time for the church and for humanity, even now irrupts into the present through the passage of the martyrs to Christ sitting at the Father's side. The "hour" of Jesus that according to St. John is his glorification and return to the right hand of the Father, is reproduced in the hour or the day of the martyr. Martyrdom is the moment of transition from the Passion to union with the risen Christ, from humiliation to glory, from temporal life to eternal life, from mortality to immortality, and at the same time it is already a realization within the present world of the Parousia and the realities of the afterlife.

The individual character of martyrdom does not conflict with the ecclesial dimension of the Parousia, for martyrdom, insofar as it unites one with Christ who is the head of the church, acquires an ecclesial dimension. [Martyrdom] is a testimony given to the

3. Ibid., 135–36.

whole church about the action of Christ in those who believe in him, a guarantee of the reality of the good things to come and a foreshadowing of Christ's coming again to bring the church to the Father.

II. OBJECTIONS FROM THE PROTESTANT CRITIQUE

The Protestant critique reproached the spirituality that formed around these martyrs, especially around St. Ignatius, for having transformed the evangelical conception of eschatology. "Whereas the Christians of the New Testament anticipated the return of Christ in glory in an eschatological vision at once transcendent and collective, Ignatius allegedly represents a true metamorphosis of eschatology on these two points. [According to the Protestant critique,] his focus on the Eucharistic sacrament and on martyrdom individualized and 'immanentized' it. That is to say, he placed in the hands of human beings the power to trigger the realization of ultimate spiritual realities, while at the same time making them an object of individual experience. This sacrament supposedly came to take the place of the Parousia, and the desire for martyrdom helped bring about the substitution of individual Christian death with the general resurrection."[4] Consider this citation from Théo Preiss: "It is true that Ignatius does not ignore the anticipation of the end of time (Eph. II, Smyrn. 9, Magn. 5). Yet let us note that Ignatius does not anticipate what Paul anticipated, [namely] God's assertion of sovereignty over the entire world, but only the definitive separation of the two worlds, which at present are still intermingled.... All the positive content of eschatology is replaced by another, ahistorical, eschatology: the

4. Father Louis Bouyer summarizes, in his own manner, the position of Théo Preiss in *L'histoire de la spiritualité chrétienne*, vol. 1, *La spiritualité du Nouveau Testament et des pères* (Paris: Les éditions du Cerf, 1960), 243.

Hellenistic concept of the soul's ascension to immortality. The prophets were resurrected by Jesus upon his coming; the martyr who imitates Christ's passion rises immediately after death. All the church is moving to God. Whether one takes the meritorious shortcut of the martyr, or follows the standard path through the church, the goal is to reach God, and the means are: the cross, that 'engine' which elevates the soul, the Holy Spirit, love and faith. Compared with that ascent to immortality, Ignatius's few eschatological reminiscences appear rather pale and conventional."[5]

In our view, these criticisms are too determined by the categories that oppose Protestants and Catholics to allow for a correct interpretation of the writings of St. Ignatius: opposition between the action of Christ who saves through faith by uniting us to his death in baptism and the action of man who seeks with his own proper capacities to adhere to Christ in his very Passion in an attempt to grasp him through a mysticism of unity. This opposition between faith in Christ and human works extends into the conception of the Parousia: on the one hand, the Parousia accomplished by Christ at the end of time in general, and on the other hand, an individual Parousia at the endpoint of mystical aspiration and effort, culminating in immortality, without much concern for history.

Such categories are, in reality, anachronistic and distort the proper proportions of the spirituality of martyrdom. One should rather interpret it in continuity with the New Testament, its direct source, while admitting that the perspectives can sometimes be too narrow or incomplete and that they fail to exhaust all the riches of Revelation. One should also remember that the spirituality of martyrdom was lived out more than it was contemplated. St. Ignatius, for instance, was not aiming to write a theological

5. See Preiss, "La mystique de l'imitation du Christ et de l'unité chez Ignace d'Antioche," *Revue d'histoire et de philosophie religieuse* 18 (1938): 226.

treatise, but only letters in which he expresses the sentiments that are animating him and that he is living out in a profound way.

For St. Ignatius, the yearning to imitate Christ in his Passion, among others, is by no means an attempt to reconstruct Christ by human effort, as one would strive to reproduce a model, but is rather the work of Christ and the Spirit in him, provoking a desire that surpasses human sentiments to the point of appearing foolish: "I endure everything because he himself, who is perfect man, empowers me."[6]

As for the Parousia, there seems to be a critical point of conjunction between it and the death of Ignatius as an encounter with Christ. Yet [this shared meeting point] in no way distorts or deemphasizes the general Parousia at the end of time. To the contrary, Ignatius saw his death as a sign and foretaste of the final Parousia (see *Letter to the Ephesians* II.1–2).

In the end, one can hardly accuse Ignatius of individualism if one considers how much emphasis he places on the unity of the church, centered on the bishop and ultimately grounded in Christ and the Father. Yet here again, we touch upon a point that awakens the suspicion of Protestant historians with respect to St. Ignatius: his testimony on behalf of the church's hierarchical structure and his insistence upon the episcopate as the foundation and sign of the unity for each [individual] church and the universal church as well.

6. "Letter of Ignatius to the Smyrnaeans," in *Apostolic Fathers*, 111.

5

THE SUMMIT OF THE SPIRITUALITY OF MARTYRDOM

The Letters of Saint Ignatius of Antioch

"The *History* of Eusebius places the martyrdom of Ignatius in the tenth year of Trajan's reign, in 107 CE, though no one really knows the source of the tradition behind this dating."[1] Joseph B. Lightfoot, at the end of a long discussion,[2] takes the date range to be 110–18 CE. Adolph von Harnack's range stops at the last years of Trajan. Thus the traditional date of 107 has value only as an approximation.[3]

The historians also discuss the authenticity of the different recensions of St. Ignatius's Letters. Father Camelot believes that in the modern recension edited in Sources chrétiennes, seven of

1. See Bardy, *La vie spirituelle d'après les Pères des trois premiers siècles*, vol. 1, p. 70ff.; Camelot, Introduction, *Ignace d'Antioche*, in Sources chrétiennes, v. 10, 10ff.

2. *Apostolic Fathers*, II.2, 435–72.

3. Camelot, Introduction, *Ignace d'Antioche*, v. 10, introduction, 12.

the letters are undoubtedly authentic. Some historians, apparently not very sympathetic with the spirituality of martyrdom when it translates into the folly of the cross, express unfavorable opinions about the content of these letters. Benjamin Aubé is one such [historian],[4] whom Jacques Moreau cites and seems to endorse:[5] "It is perhaps difficult to say that everything here is fabricated and freely invented , but it is also not easy to maintain that there is a single [letter] in which the pious imagination of the subsequent generation did not leave its mark." In reference to the passage from [Ignatius's] Letter to the Romans (V.2), "I will flatter the beasts," Aubé wrote; "This frenetic appeal to death, and not only to a simple death, but to the most refined of tortures, [is] too curiously articulated not to be a fabricated exaltation."[6]

Whatever these discussions where the opinions of historians sometimes play a greater role than the texts themselves, the Letters of St. Ignatius, and particularly his letter to the Romans, nonetheless represent the summit of the Christian spirituality of martyrdom. Understanding them clearly requires a certain sensibility with respect to the Christian faith, since here we encounter the love of the cross and of Christ expressed in its purest form. Such sentiments can only seem crazy or fanciful from the perspective of worldly good sense. The fact remains, however, that these letters provide us with a glimpse of the profound depths and inspirations of the Christian soul as it advances toward martyrdom. These writings of Ignatius thus provide a happy complement to the acts of the martyrs from this era, which generally tend to recount events more than they express the movements of the soul.

4. Benjamin Aubé, *Histoire des persécutions de l'église jusqu'à la fin des Antonins* (Paris: Librairie Academique, 1875).

5. Jacques Moreau, *La persécution du christianisme dans l'Empire romain* (Paris: Presses universitaires de France, 1956), 46 and 40.

6. Cited by Henri Grégoire, *Les persecutions dans l'Empire romain* (Brussels: Palais des Académies, 1964), 106.

The main passage from the Letter to the Romans that will be of particular interest to us [in this regard] is in chapters II through VIII. Let us present a brief account of it.

The text consists, as it were, of six successive waves expressing Ignatius's desire: they depart from different points, but each time return with force to the same central idea, expressed in [St. Paul's] Letter to the Philippians (Phil 1:23): "my desire is to depart and be with Christ, for that is far better." Or again, it is like a musical theme where the same movement is repeated with variations that each reinforce a central melody.

The theme commences with a brief introduction that encapsulates the whole: the fear expressed by Ignatius that the Christians of Rome, through what he considers to be a misguided love, may try to prevent him from suffering martyrdom. "I fear that your charity may do me harm. Since for you it is easy to do what you want; but for me it is difficult to attain God, unless you spare me." We must situate this sentence in the broader reality of a crucial experience for a man: the concrete perspective of death, with a heightened awareness of an unfolding opportunity to escape. Instead of seizing that opportunity, Ignatius demands and begs that the Romans do nothing to save him, since in his eyes death is the path to God, to true life. He thus inverts the meaning of all the terms he uses. The charity that leads one to do good and to endeavor to preserve another's life, causes harm according to Ignatius, if it seeks to save him from death, and does good only if it allows him to die so that he might attain true life. For Ignatius, deliverance consists not in being spared death, but in being allowed to go to death.

One can understand how this reversal of values with respect to life would seem insane to those without faith. What is expressed here is indeed either madness or the supreme wisdom of the cross, which, as we remarked, cannot be attained by human initiative, but only by the prompting of the Holy Spirit.

The first wave (chapter II) relies upon the Romans' felt desire to please God: in Ignatius's case, the best way [they can do that] is to keep their silence. Did not St. Paul say, "Am I now seeking human approval, or God's approval? Or am I trying to please people? If I were still pleasing people, I would not be a servant of Christ" (Gal 1:9–10)? Ignatius comes to describe martyrdom as a liturgy: "Grant me nothing more than to be poured out as an offering to God while the altar is ready." St. Paul writes something similar to the Philippians: "But even if I am being poured out as a libation over the sacrifice and the offering of your faith, I am glad and rejoice with all of you" (Phil 2:17). He likewise addresses the Romans, "I appeal to you therefore, brothers and sisters, by the mercies of God, to present your bodies as a living sacrifice, holy and acceptable to God, which is your spiritual worship" (Rom 12:1).

The second wave begins with an allusion to the Letter of Clement of Rome to the Corinthians, whose overriding injunction is to avoid jealousy, the cause of all sins against Christ (Letter of Clement, III–VI). Ignatius returns this lesson to the Romans: that they not be jealous of him, [nor] of the grace by which he walks, and that they instead pray for him, so that he may have the internal and external strength to speak out and desire to be a true believer, which will come to pass only as he disappears before the eyes of the world to see Christ. This is the theme of entering into the invisible, into the mystery of the Father, likewise present in St. Paul: "We speak God's wisdom, secret and hidden" (1 Cor 2:7). "Set your minds on things that are above, not on things that are on earth, for you have died, and your life is hidden with Christ in God" (Col 3:2–3).

The third wave begins with letters written to other churches and is summed up in the affirmation that "I die for God of my own free will," which acquires its greatest force in his plea [to] "let me be food for the wild beasts, through whom I can reach God. I am God's wheat, and I am being ground by the teeth of the wild beasts, that I might prove to be pure bread." Ignatius will thus become a true disciple of Jesus Christ, a victim offered to God, who disappears in him with the hope of being reborn free in Christ: "If I suffer, I will be a freedman of Jesus Christ, and will rise up free in him." "But now," writes St. Paul, "that you have been freed from sin and enslaved to God, the advantage you get is sanctification. The end is eternal life" (Rom 6:22).

The fourth wave mentions the torments already suffered at the hands of the soldiers who guard him: "From Syria to Rome I battle the beasts, on land and on sea, by night and by day, chained to ten leopards, that is to say a detachment of soldiers; who become worse whenever it suits them." He thinks about the impending torture, which becomes desirable through his yearning to find Christ: that nothing, not jealousy of the Romans nor even that of the beasts, nothing visible or invisible, might prevent him from being a disciple by joining Christ beyond the threshold of death.

The fifth wave begins with his detachment from the world and seeks to describe how much greater, by contrast, is the attractiveness of Christ. "The charms of the world and the kingdoms of this age are no longer of any use to me. It is better for me to die so as to unite myself to Christ Jesus than to rule over the ends of the earth. I seek him who died for us; I desire him who was risen for us. My birth approaches." In the light of the Resurrection, death appears to him as a birth into life, hence the inversion: life equals death and death equals life. As it is for St. Paul as well: "For to me, living is Christ and dying is gain … my desire is to depart and be with Christ, for that is far better" (Phil 1:21–23). At last the theme of the imitation of Christ makes itself heard: "Allow me to be an imitator of the passion of our Lord. If anyone has God in him, then he understands what it is I desire, and he will have compassion on me, knowing what it is that has taken hold of me." The sixth wave proceeds by confronting the prince of this world and his envy, which the Roman church must not share, so as to bring into relief the substance of the martyr's desire: "There is no more fire of material longing within me, but only water living and speaking in me: 'Come to the Father.'"[7] This is why he no longer has any other hunger but for the flesh and blood of Christ, for his incorruptible love. Concerning the statement "my *eros* has been crucified," the most frequent interpretation since Origen was to identify this *eros*, this love, with Christ: "My love (Christ) has been crucified." Father Camelot prefers to construe this term as designating earthly desires and translates [the phrase as] "my earthly desire has been crucified."[8]

All these movements culminate in a more compact conclusion: "I no longer want to live according to human standards.... Pray for me, that I may reach the goal.... If I suffer, you will have wanted it; if I am rejected, you will have hated me."[9]

Surely we encounter here the summit of the spirituality of martyrdom, and indeed of Christian mysticism in every age. These texts are profoundly evangelical: centered on Christ, and animated by the yearning to be with him, implying a personal journey through the Passion so as to attain true life. They are also trinitarian: the inspiration comes from the Holy Spirit, the living water that calls one to go to the Father; such is the sentiment of Jesus himself, who desired with a great desire to go to the Father.

Note the realism of this letter, which has already appeared to us in the retort to the Docetists and which is affirmed here with extreme force in the face of approaching torture. [This realism] stands out in this [particular] situation: one can hardly compose

7. "Letter of Ignatius to the Romans," in *Apostolic Fathers*, 105.

8. On this phrase "my *eros* has been crucified," see Camelot, Introduction, *Ignace d'Antioche*, v. 10, 134–35.

9. "Letter of Ignatius to the Romans," 105.

pious literature when one is in the power of cruel guards awaiting torture, especially at the moment when one glimpses an imminent opportunity to escape. Let us note also the idea that one truly becomes a Christian and a disciple of Jesus only when one has passed through suffering and death.

The Letter to the Romans powerfully expresses one of the two essential dimensions of any Christian spirituality, as expressed in St. Paul's double expression in the Letter to the Philippians (Phil 1:22–24): the desire to go and be with Christ and the obedience to remain in the flesh for the good of other Christians. That latter dimension expresses itself in Ignatius's concern for the churches of Asia to whom he writes. The former is especially manifest in the Letter to the Romans, a result of the immediate prospect of martyrdom, seen by him as a unique and reliable occasion to go to Christ. One can find here the fundamental themes of Christian spirituality: the action of the Holy Spirit and of *agape* centered on the Eucharist, such that it provokes a desire that transforms the vision of death and provides strength to desire [death] in spite of human weakness and fear of failure; martyrdom understood as the model paradigm of spiritual combat against the devil, with its temptations and its torments, [a combat] that must be waged through the asceticism of faith in Christ, in imitation of his sufferings, and granting victory over carnal desires; the spiritual begetting that gives birth to the new man, freed by faith and love from the bondage to the passions and servitude to the devil, and made into a servant of justice, in opposition to the old man and to the world where the desires of the flesh reign [supreme]; the desire to be hidden in Christ, in the secret of the Father; and the march to the endpoint and the epicenter of life, firmly located in the risen Christ, beyond this existence.

6

CLEMENT OF ROME'S *LETTER TO THE CORINTHIANS*

The Letter of St. Clement of Rome to the Christians at Corinth is, apart from the writings of the New Testament, the most ancient piece of Christian literature whose authorship, location, and dating are historically certain. This letter is so beautiful and so rich that it was long read by many churches during the Eucharistic liturgy.[1]

The letter was occasioned by the grave troubles in the Church of Corinth, where a faction had risen up against the presbyters and had deposed them. It speaks of the persecution of Nero and makes allusion to a second persecution with which it was contemporaneous, that of Domitian in the years 95 and 96 CE "These are the misfortunes and the trials with which we have been suddenly hit in quick succession, and which have, by necessary discretion, kept us for so long from turning to you, good friends, to settle

1. Bardy, *La vie spirituelle*, 1:102ff.; Quasten, *Initiation aux Pères de l'Église*, 1:52ff.

the matter in dispute among you: this sedition which has neither right nor place among the elect of God."

The purpose of the letter is certainly not to recount the events of the persecution in Rome, but it contains a long and beautiful prayer that reveals to us the state of the Christian soul with regard to the Roman authorities, even as they were suffering persecution from them:

> Give concord and peace
> to us and to all the inhabitants of the earth,
> just as you did to our fathers
> who called upon you in faith and in truth,
> subject to your omnipotence and your holiness.
> It is you, sovereign Master, who
> by your marvelous and ineffable strength,
> have given power and dominion
> to the princes and authorities of the earth.
> We therefore remain subject to them,
> recognizing the glory and honor
> which you have vested in them,
> so that we might not contradict your will.
> Grant them, Lord,
> health, peace, harmony and stability,
> that they might exercise without error
> the sovereignty which you have bestowed upon them.
> For it is you, heavenly Master and King of the ages,
> Who dispense to the children of men
> glory, honor and power
> over the things of the earth;
> direct, Lord, their counsel,
> according to what is good and pleasing in your sight,
> so that in exercising
> with piety, peace and meekness

the power which you have given them,
they might experience your favor.
You alone have the power to accomplish these things,
and to bring about still greater ones.
We give you thanks for the high priest
and guardian of our souls, Jesus Christ,
through whom all glory and majesty are yours,
now and for all generations,
and unto the ages of ages. Amen.

This prayer comes directly from the precept of the Sermon on the Mount: "love your enemies, and pray for those who persecute you" (Mt 5:44). It implies, with regard to the authorities, the affirmation that power comes from God, who directs the counsel of the authorities in order that they might obtain his grace. "It is you, sovereign Master, who by your marvelous and ineffable strength, have given power and dominion to the princes and authorities of the earth. We therefore remain subject to them, recognizing the glory and honor which you have vested in them, so that we might not contradict your will." Then comes the petition for health and peace: "Grant them, Lord. . . ." And with regard to Christians, it lifts up the prayer to be delivered from those who pursue them with an unjust hatred, [and] to be subject both to the divine name and to those who govern them: "Show us your face, O Sovereign Master, that we may partake of your bounty in peace; protect us by your powerful hand, free us from all sin by your sovereign arm, and save us from those who hate us unjustly."

What gives this prayer its full dimension is that it is not only personal, but authentically ecclesial and liturgical, as well. We are dealing here with a time in which the formulas of the Christian liturgy have yet to be definitely established, when those who presided over the assemblies still enjoyed sufficient liberty to lead and compose prayer. As Chanoine Bardy notes, the pace, the fullness, and the themes of the prayers in St. Clement's Letter are very liturgical in style, and indeed the themes are taken up by subsequent liturgies: the grandeur of God in his works, the beauty of creation, the multitude of heavenly hosts who surround the throne of the Lord, and the inestimable blessing of the redemption. "One senses that we are witnessing here the first emergence of the official prayer of the Church."

It is within this rich framework that the prayer for the authorities is inscribed, even during times of persecution. These are the sentiments of the church of God that St. Clement expresses with serenity and solemnity. They confer a new amplitude upon St. Paul's thought that all power comes from God and upon St. Peter's injunction to honor the emperor: he prays for all those who govern the world in spite of their attacks against the church.

This prayer is marked by a sovereign serenity because it is composed in the sight of God, who controls human history and freely distributes his mercy to all, particularly to those who recognize the name of Jesus Christ, the Savior. In order to appreciate this peaceful tone, one need only read over Roman historians such as Suetonius and Tacitus, who amply portray how callous and even brutal the exercise of power could be in Rome, as well as how bitter the struggle was to obtain it.

[In conclusion], let us add a passage from the Letter of Polycarp of Smyrna to the Philippians written in the same tone: "Pray also for the kings, for the authorities and for the princes, and for those who persecute you and hate you, and for the enemies of the cross; in this way the fruit that you bear will be visible to all, and you will be made perfect in him" (XII.2).

7

TERTULLIAN

The Treatise *Ad Martyras*

The treatise *Ad Martyras* is usually dated to the year 197 CE. Born between 150 and 160 CE, Tertullian was converted around 195 CE and immediately began a series of apologetic works. *Ad martyras* is one of his first works.[1] Quasten writes, "It is assumed that Perpetua and Felicity could have belonged to a group of confessors who perused this treatise. Both of them, indeed, were catechumens and died for their faith in 202 CE. The work would thus date back to that same year. The *Passio Perpetuae et Felicitatis* and the treatise *Ad martyras* have so many commonalities that the authorship of both was attributed to Tertullian." Yet this is only one hypothesis; the style so characteristic of Tertullian is not found in the *Passion of Perpetua and Felicity*, [and] the very title of the treatise poses a problem. The Latin should be rendered *Ad martyres*. *Ad martyras*

1. Quasten, *Initiation aux Pères de l'Église*, 2:344, 347; Bardy, *La vie spirituelle*, 2:163–76; R. Braun, "Sur la date, la composition et le text de l'*Ad Martyras* de Tertullien," *Rev. Et. August.* 24 (1978): 221–24.

could be a transcription from Greek, in that *martus* can be masculine, feminine, or neuter.

The treatise begins with a brief introduction. Tertullian proposes, despite his personal unworthiness, to bring spiritual nourishment to the martyrs who receive bodily nourishment from the church and from other Christians.

I. THE PRISON AS THE SITE OF SPIRITUAL COMBAT

Tertullian starts with a veritable meditation on prison by presenting it as the site of the spiritual combat that the martyrs wage against the devil, under the guidance of the Holy Spirit. It is the Holy Spirit who has led them into prison, into the den of the devil, so that they might vanquish him: "Do not grieve the Holy Spirit [see Eph 4:30] who has entered with you into prison. Indeed, if he had not entered with you, you would not be there today. Make sure that he remains with you and brings you to the Lord."

With one phrase, Tertullian defines an entire conception of martyrdom. It was not the soldiers of the proconsul, but the Spirit of God who led the martyrs into prison. This sojourn is a passage through temptation and leads to Christ. One cannot help but think here of the entrance of Christ into the desert under the movement of the Spirit in order to be tempted by the devil. This theme will be taken up subsequently by monasticism, which made the desert the site of combat against the devil.

Note the sense of the active presence of the Holy Spirit that accompanies the martyrs in prison. In the Acts of the Martyrs of Lyon and Smyrna, the presence of Christ is specified instead. It would be going too far, it seems to us, to perceive a Montanist influence here, as some historians have done.

The assistance of the Holy Spirit is all the more necessary insofar as prison presents itself as the domain of the devil: "Prison is the house of the devil, where he guards his family." And Tertullian attributes to him these words: "They are among me, and I test them with depraved hatred, with defections and with dissension."

Why is prison the house of the devil? Certainly it is the place where one confines criminals; but it is above all the site where the Roman authorities unjustly incarcerate, as convicts, those who bear the name of Christ, and where they undergo their first test. Prison thus takes on a kind of spiritual significance and becomes the place where the faithful are tested in the claws of the devil.

Tertullian consequently shows Christians that they have been led into prison in order to vanquish the spirit of evil and, first on this point, to resist the temptation to divide and oppose one another [and] to maintain concord and peace among themselves. Notice the vigorous expression: "For your peace is to him a war." This peace between them will allow them to reconcile truthfully with those who, having apostatized, now come to them seeking communion with the church, as was a frequent practice.

Note that this theme of peace reappears in monasticism: in his battle against the devil, the monk must make sure to guard the peace of heart that will then emanate from him. In Tertullian, this peace is the peace of Christians among themselves and within the church. Such are the fruits of the Spirit according to St. Paul: charity, joy, peace, gentleness (Gal 5:22).

II. LIBERATION FROM THE TRUE PRISON OF THE WORLD

Through a reversal of perspectives, the prison theme then develops into that of separation from the world and its bonds, including even familial bonds: "if we really reflect on the fact that the world itself is the real prison, then we come to understand that you have come out of prison rather than having entered it."

1. Tertullian defends this bold assertion: the world contains greater shadows that darken the hearts of men, heavier chains that bind their souls, and more repulsive filth, such as the passions of men. The world is made up of more malefactors—that is to say, the entire human race (see Rom 1–2: "All are sinners and are in need of the redemption of Christ"), and is under the judgment of God himself.

However, amid these shadows, Christians are the light (see Mt 5:14; 1 Thes 5:5; Eph 5:8: "You were once darkness, but now you are light in the Lord"). They also fill this realm with a fragrant aroma (see Ez 20:41; Eph 5:2; 2 Cor 2:15: "for we are to God the fragrance of Christ among those who are being saved and among those who are lost"). And ultimately, they will act as judges over those who have judged them (Ws 3:8; 1 Cor 6:2: *Do you not know that the saints shall judge the world?*)[2] To the Christian who has renounced the world and is leaving this age, the place one happens to occupy in that realm matters little.

Tertullian achieves a remarkable transposition here from the prison theme to the level of the heart, where matters are reversed. The true prison is in the heart of man, where the darkness of sin and impurity reign; there we find the true bondage of those awaiting God's judgment. Hence we can say that the world is more truly a prison than the location where the martyrs are confined.

In contrast, true freedom is freedom for God who reigns in the heart of the martyrs, with their light and interior fragrance, and the assurance that exonerates them from the judgment of the world.

This idea is not the restating of the Platonic notion that considers the body to be a tomb (*soma-sèma*) and would lead to the

2. Here Pinckaers is summarizing the general point of the various scriptural passages he has just cited [Tr.].

quest for disembodiment. Tertullian is too realistic and too Latin to entertain such a view. If the world is a prison, it is on account of the sin that resides in man and that makes the world a prison under the control of the devil. The martyrs then become free by abandoning the world and entering into prison.

Here one may recall the passage from St. Paul that says, "Just as you once presented your members as slaves to impurity and to greater and greater iniquity, so now present your members as slaves to righteousness for sanctification. When you were slaves of sin, you were free with regard to righteousness.... But now that you have been freed from sin and enslaved to God, the advantage you get is sanctification. The end is eternal life" (Rom 6:19–23). One may likewise think of the significance that captivity and imprisonment have for St. Paul: "our struggle is not against enemies of blood and flesh, but ... against the rulers of this present darkness, against the spiritual forces of evil.... Pray in the Spirit at all times ... (that I may be able to) make known with boldness the mystery of the Gospel for which I am an ambassador in chains" (Eph 6:12–20).

We also rediscover this theme in monasticism, when St. Anthony goes to dwell in an old fort in the middle of the desert, as a voluntary prisoner of Christ, where he will win his freedom and attain interior light.

2. The theme continues under another aspect: the admission into prison is a kind of negotiation where one exchanges the joys of this life for other joys in which the spirit gains much more than the flesh loses. Setting aside God's promises to the martyrs, a topic about which he seems to suggest he will speak more later (in a section of the letter that is apparently lost to us now), Tertullian enumerates the advantages that the martyrs enjoy in prison. Their bodies do not lack the necessary grace to care for their brothers, and their spirits obtain the blessings of faith, which are always of use.

Negatively speaking, they no longer have before their eyes the depraved spectacles that one could not avoid in the world: the images of gods and the crowd that honors them, the clamors of cruel spectacles, or the display of shamelessness. The martyrs are freed from all these temptations that assail Christians.

Positively speaking, in a word: the prison procures for the Christian what the desert was for the prophets, [a place] where one can see an allusion to Elijah (1 Kgs 19:4). In this vein, Tertullian evokes the Lord's love of solitary places, where he would retire to pray and where he manifested his glory to his disciples during the Transfiguration. And so he proposes replacing the term "prison" with "retreat." In this retreat, the spirit discovers its proper space in which it will complete its journey to God.

The spiritual space that Tertullian offers to martyrs is not that of dialogue, questioning, or philosophical contemplation, examples of which we find in Plato's *Crito*, which portrays Socrates conversing with his friends before drinking the hemlock, or [even] later in Boethius's *Consolation of Philosophy*. One must clearly glimpse this spiritual space from the evangelical perspective opened up to us by the Holy Spirit—that is to say, by attentive meditation on the Word of God and by prayer in conjunction with a concrete consideration of the Christian's condition in the world and amid this trial, of which the following will give an example.

It is in this spiritual space that the whole contemplative dimension of subsequent Christian tradition unfolds, especially that of the Greek [fathers], St. Augustine and the mystics. Yet Tertullian remains closer to the realm of the martyrs' experience with his external focus on the prison, the tribunal, and the arena that await them. His reflection is not any less spiritual.

The explicit relation established between the prison and the desert explicitly evokes the theme of the desert as it will develop later. Elijah, the archetype of the prophet who resides in the desert and journeys to Horeb to encounter God, will be the model for

Anthony, the father of monasticism. Tertullian's phrase establishes in advance the link between the spirituality of martyrdom and monastic spirituality.

III. THE MARTYRS AS SOLDIERS AND ATHLETES FOR CHRIST

Opening up a third perspective, Tertullian sees in the prison the training ground of soldiers for Christ, the *palestra* where Christian athletes exercise. Let us think of prison as a training ground. Tertullian introduces this theme of "the militia for Christ" by comparing the severity of prison life to the austere life that soldiers lead in camp, even in times of peace, in order to condition themselves for the necessities of wartime. He then makes an imperceptible transition from military combat to combat in the stadium when he says [that] martyrs should harden themselves with the exercise of spiritual and corporal virtue, and [so] should prepare themselves to fight the good fight that awaits them, in which God is the commissioner of the games and the Holy Spirit is the trainer, and after which they shall receive the crown of eternity.

It should be noted that Tertullian transposes all the vocabulary related to gaming in this passage from Greek to Latin, since Latin did not have these technical terms. One only comes across one Latin word: *disciplina*—teaching, education, military training—instead of the Greek term *askèsis* (rendered as *asceticism* in [English]), which designates the gymnastic exercises that were a regular part of athletic life.

Thus Christ sets the martyrs apart so as to train them in the discipline of athletes: the more they struggle, the more they will be able to hope for victory, on account of their courage.

Here again, we find themes that will return in subsequent monastic and religious spiritualities. The Christian is similar to a soldier or an athlete who trains for spiritual combat. For the martyrs, the training site is the prison; for the monks, it will be the desert. The theme of the militia of Christ will be taken up again by St. Benedict and St. Ignatius of Loyola. It will comprise the important roles of asceticism and discipline in monastic spirituality.

We should also take note of the fundamentally Christian character of the theme presented here: the exercises are presided over by the Holy Spirit, and Christ is their head. Therefore it is in faith, prompted by the Holy Spirit and grace, that one may wage such combat and perform the exercises that are necessary for it. We have not made a simple Christian transposition from the realm of human virtue sustained by natural powers, as the philosophers would teach us. Likewise, the theme of discipline or asceticism should be understood as the striving for spiritual progress conforming to the teaching of Christ, carried out under the guidance of the Spirit [and] in the sight of the Father who sees in secret. For Tertullian, the term *discipline* does not designate penitential practices, but rather the exercises necessary to advance in virtue.

We would also do well to highlight the strength of Tertullian's Christian intuition in taking full account of the harsh realism of the situation in which he writes. It takes a very strong vision of faith to perceive in the Roman judge and those who serve him the action of God, Christ, and the Holy Spirit. This transformative vision of faith is similar to that of the evangelists when they show us, in the Passion of Jesus, handed over to the Sanhedrin and the power of Pilate, the accomplishment of the Father's will, and [when they] convey to us the silent sovereignty of Jesus who submits to them.

IV. FIGHTING FOR THE SPIRIT, STRENGTHENING THE FLESH

The exhortation begins at the Lord's words, which the martyrs experienced firsthand: "the spirit is willing, but the flesh is weak"

(Mt 26:42). Yet since Tertullian does not want this saying to become a possible excuse for their weakness, he interprets it in a way that corresponds to his goal, as the Lord's indicating that the weaker element, the flesh, should serve the stronger—namely, the spirit—and that the spirit in turn should strengthen the flesh by preparing for battle. In order to demonstrate how the spirit can prevail amid the torments of death despite the fears of the flesh, Tertullian then presents a series of examples of celebrated men and women from antiquity. Here is a brief historical exposition of each of these figures: *Lucretius*: daughter of Spurius Lucretius, prefect of Rome, wife of Tarquinius Collantinus. According to the tradition reported by Titus Livius, she was raped by Sextus, son of Tarquinius Superbus, and killed herself in front of her family, asking them for vengeance. This drama allegedly incited the overthrow of the monarchy and the establishment of the republic. *Dido*: placed by Virgil at the time of the Aeneid and the Trojan War, she threw herself upon a pyre and stabbed herself with a dagger in order to escape the prosecution of Iarbas, a local king who wanted to force her into marriage. *Mucius Scaevola* (second century CE), whose name means "lefty": a prisoner, he burned his own right hand on a brazier and frightened his enemies with his courage. *Heraclitus of Ephesus*, an eminent philosopher from the early fifth century CE: after being overwhelmed by the early onset of aging, he allowed himself to die of hunger at the age of 60. His misanthropic temperament inspired the legend that he perpetually wept. *Empedocles of Agrigento* (d. 430 CE) reputedly ended his own life by throwing himself into the crater of Mt. Aetna. *Peregrinus Proteus*, a cynic philosopher and sometime Christian before taking up the mantle of philosophy: he was exiled from Rome for having denounced Marcus Aurelius, fled to Greece, and there solemnly immolated himself at the Olympic games of 165 CE. Lucian wrote *The Death of Peregrinus* in 169 CE in order to ridicule Cynicism and Christianity. *Regulus Marcus Attilius* (d. 250 CE): a prisoner of the Carthaginians, he was released in order to negotiate a prisoner exchange with Rome on the condition that he afterward return to Carthage. After dissuading the Romans from consenting to a shameful peace, he then returned voluntarily to the custody of the Carthaginians on account of his oath, and was subsequently tortured to death. And finally, *Cleopatra* (d. 30 CE), the renowned queen of Egypt, who upon seeing that Octavian, the future Augustus, would take her to Rome to appear in his triumph, committed suicide at the age of 36 by allowing an asp to bite her arm.

Tertullian does not relate these well-known examples to present them to the Christians as models that he would have been better off taking from scripture, but rather in order to establish the premise of an a fortiori argument: if these men and women accepted agonizing deaths for the sake of human praise and vainglory, should not [death and agony] appear more insignificant to Christians, who desire heavenly glory and a divine recompense? If these pagans paid so much for a glass pearl, how much more should Christians be willing to give for a real one[?] We have here a strong expression of Christian fortitude in the face of suffering and death, one that portrays it as surpassing human courage, even in spite of the weakness of the flesh.

V. FINAL EXHORTATION

This exhortation is followed by the remark that, through a sort of disease, some feel an attraction that leads them to disregard pain and to confront dangers, beasts, and fire. God has permitted these abilities in order to encourage us and shame us if we should refuse to suffer for the truth and for salvation what these people endure on account of vanity and to their loss.

The exhortation ends by building upon a simple observation of the human condition: have not many people died in fires, or been killed by beasts, brigands, or enemies? That which we hesitate to suffer for the cause of God, every man could be led to suffer for a human cause, whether voluntarily or not. The last words of the treatise may be an allusion to the Battle of Lyon, in which Albinus, the commanding general of Britain, was killed by Septimus Severus as a usurper on February 19, 197CE.

Although these observations may appear trivial, they are nonetheless true and make us aware of the fragility of things. One such reflection takes on [more] power at the moment in which man is tempted to cling desperately to life. These themes [and] the [practice of] meditating on the fragility of life and on death in order to reinforce Christian courage will reappear in monasticism and in subsequent spiritualities. Note finally that the work ends *ex abrupto*, without a conclusion, which gives rise to the belief that the text we now possess is incomplete.

Conclusion

The *Ad martyras* of Tertullian, in spite of its brevity, is an astonishingly rich text in the themes it expresses in dense, compact phrases. It always remains grounded in concrete realities, but its thoughts are developed with profundity and vigor. Tertullian outlines here the principal characteristics of the Christian soul, as one will later discover them in subsequent spiritualities, particularly that of monasticism. In this sense, one could say that it is a prophetic work. One should therefore not be surprised by its success in the Christian tradition. As Quasten writes, "despite its brevity (only 6 chapters) and the simplicity of its style, it has won the sustained admiration of successive generations."[3]

3. Quasten, *Patrology,* v.II, 290.

8

THE SPIRITUALITY OF MARTYRDOM IN ST. AUGUSTINE

With St. Augustine, we move beyond the time of persecutions, [beyond] that era in which the history of the church was dominated by the ideal of martyrdom, and enter into a period in which Christian thought and spirituality blossom in new directions: the monastic spirituality of St. Anthony, the contemplative spirituality of the Greek fathers, and the sapiential spirituality of St. Augustine. However, the latter is still near enough the time of persecutions that ended at the beginning of his century, fifty years before his birth, for it to linger in his memory, owing above all to the memory of the Christian people who remained engrossed by the martyrs' struggles and to the liturgy that commemorated their anniversaries and venerated their relics. Augustine himself was present in Milan in 386 CE when St. Ambrose discovered the bodies of the martyrs Gervasius and Protasius, and as bishop he was [later] prompted to preach numerous sermons on the feasts of martyrs, when he would disclose his own thoughts about the nature and meaning of their combat. St. Augustine, then, is a good witness to the way in which the spirituality of martyrdom undergoes a transition between the era of persecution and the development of the new ideal of Christian holiness, an ideal that he himself helped to shape.

THE TEXTS

In the work of St. Augustine, the principal texts on martyrdom are found in the sermons he preached on the feasts of the martyrs. One can also find some passages in his commentaries on the *Psalms* and in *De civitate Dei* and *De trinitate*, [but] the main bulk of them are in the sermons.

We should remember that these sermons are actually transcriptions, though one can clearly recognize in them Augustine's style and mode of thought.

The dating of the sermons is not always precise or even established. [Much of] what we have comes to us from Pierre-Patrick Verbraken.[1] Without getting into too much detail, we shall indicate our preference for Kunzelmann's dating. Here is the list of Augustine's principal sermons on the martyrs with their current dating: Sermon 273, on the feasts of Ss. Fructuosus, Augurius, and Eulogius, 396 CE, at Hippo; sermons 274 to 277, on the feast of St. Vincent, 410–13 CE; sermons 280 to 282: March 7, 412–16 CE; Sermon 283, 412–16 CE; Sermon 284: May 8, 418 CE; Sermon 285, 416 CE; Sermon 286: June 9, sometime around 425 CE.

On St. Lawrence: Sermon 302, circa 400 CE; Sermon 303, 425–30 CE; Sermon 304: after 417 CE; Sermon 305: before 417 CE.

On St. Cyprian: sermons 309 and 310, at Carthage, Sermon

1. See Pierre-Patrick Verbraken, *Études critiques sur les Sermons authentiques de saint Augustin*, vol. 2, Instrumenta patristica 3 (Steenbrugge: 1976).

311, at Carthage, in 401–5 CE; Sermon 312: at Carthage, around 417 CE Sermon 313.

On St. Stephen: Sermon 314, before 425 CE; Sermon 315, Eastertide of 416–17 CE at Hippo; Sermon 316, Eastertide of 425 CE at the earliest; Sermon 317, at Hippo, possibly in 424 or 425 CE; Sermon 318, around 425 CE; Sermon 319, 425 CE at the earliest.

Sermon 325: November 15, 405–411 CE; Sermon 326: November 15; Sermon 327, 405–11 CE; Sermon 328, 405–11 CE; Sermon 329, 410–12 CE; Sermon 330: August 18, 397 CE; Sermon 331, sometime in the summer; Sermon 332, 410–12 CE; Sermon 333: usage of a lost sermon; Sermon 334: August 6; Sermon 335: 410–12 CE. The question of the dating of the sermons is only of relative importance for us, although we do sometimes sense the clear influence of current preoccupations, particularly those surrounding the Donatist and the Pelagian controversies beginning in 411 CE

We will organize the teaching of the sermons on the martyrs according to five themes that express their most fundamental aspects.

I. THE TESTIMONY OF MARTYRDOM

St. Augustine knows the etymology of the term *martyr* and begins with it in Sermon 286, on the feast of Ss. Gervasius and Protasius, whose lives are unknown but who became famous because of the discovery of their relics by St. Ambrose in Milan.[2] "The name of martyr," says St. Augustine, "is a Greek term, but its usage has passed into the Latin language and its meaning is 'witness' (*testis*)."

Thus by Augustine's time, the term *martyr* had entered into Latin usage with its Christian meaning, and it became important to remind the people of the primitive sense of the word.

Augustine's commentary on the First Epistle of St. John demonstrates this point: "Some of us brothers who do not know

2. See Augustine, *Confessions* 1.IX.VII.16

Greek may not know which Greek term corresponds to our word 'witness' (*testis* is used to translate the Greek word *martyroumen* in the Latin version of St. John's text). It is a term familiar to all, and one that has taken on a specifically religious meaning; in fact, those whom we call *witnesses* in Latin are called *martyrs* in the Greek" (1 Jn 1:2).

[Augustine's] sermon begins with this original etymology in order to develop an account of testimony and discern what a martyr truly is. True witnesses must be distinguished from false ones. Martyrs are truthful witnesses worthy of the crown, not false witnesses who merit punishment. This distinction is not [yet fully] developed in the account given by our sermon, but insofar as "true witness" implies "witness to the truth," it will be brought out more clearly by the claim that one merits the title of martyr principally on account of the cause to which one bears witness.

Among witnesses to the truth, one may distinguish three degrees:

1. Hidden witnesses: the Jews who believed in Jesus but did not dare confess it publicly (Joseph of Arimathea and Nicodemus, for example, as related by 1 John 19:38–39), preferring the glory of men to that of God. Their testimony is but a whisper.

2. Those who had the courage to confess Christ before men, but who were unable to maintain their confession to the point of death. Such was the case with Peter during the Passion.

3. Those who were ready to confess Christ to the point of dying for him. Such is the perfect form of testimony, to which one can add nothing, and which constitutes the most proper definition of martyrdom.

St. Augustine illustrates this distinction of degrees, particularly between the last two, through the contradistinction of St. Peter and the martyrs Gervasius and Protaseus. This comparison allows him to demonstrate that martyrdom is above all a work of grace. Peter, during the life of Christ, had given public testimony to him when he was sent on mission; he was already an apostle. He had also confessed Christ on behalf of the twelve, and he had heard it said to him, "You are Peter and on this rock I will build my Church" (Mt 16:18). However, he had not yet reached the degree of testimony given by Gervasius and Protasius, [or] by Stephen, [or] by a child, like Nemesianus, [or] by a young woman like Crispina or Agnes.

Where does the difference lie? It lies in the fact that Peter, overly sure of his own strength and ignorant of his weakness, desired even to pass before Christ on the way of death (Mt 26:33; 1 Jn 13:37–38). Like a latent disease, his weakness was revealed at the moment when he had to bear witness before a simple servant who asked him, *Are you one of them?* (Mt 26:73). At that instant, the fever rose in him and led him to that true death, which is the denial of Christ, who is true life. [We see here] the complete failure of that initial good intention that was leading Peter toward witness and martyrdom. Because of his presumption his apostolic testimony resulted in denial.

Yet Christ's mere glance was sufficient to initiate Peter's healing: "the Lord looked at him, and Peter began to weep bitterly" (Lk 22:61–62). The repentance of Peter leads to a true resurrection, which Augustine forcefully articulates: "in denying, he died; in weeping, he rose again. *Negando periit, flendo resurrexit.*" More precisely, it was necessary that Christ should die first so that Peter could follow the path now laid open of testimony unto death, the way of martyrdom on which Peter would subsequently walk together with the other apostles, and where the [other] martyrs would later follow.

Martyrdom is therefore unattainable to those who rely on their own strength. It is only possible as a result of the death of

Christ for his disciples, which opens up this path to them and makes it viable. The Passion of Jesus is thus the testimony par excellence. The martyrdom of Christians is an imitation of Christ.

Augustine also specifies the most prominent and efficacious element of the testimony of the martyrs: it was not their words so much as their actions, their death more so than their life, in accordance with the line from Psalm 115 that declares "precious in the eyes of the Lord is the death of his faithful ones." By this death, cherished by God and despised by the men of the current age, the martyrs become the seed that gives rise to the church's fecundity: "The earth was filled with the blood of the martyrs as with a precious seed, and this seed has produced the rich harvest of the Church." The death of the martyrs also participates in the fecundity of the Passion of Christ. Today the shame of the martyrs has turned into honor in the eyes of the now Christianized world. St. Augustine also adds that a Christian can be a martyr in his bed, if he remains faithful to Christ in the face of disease and death, refusing the amulets and superstitions that some hold out to him.

Sermon 328 (from between 405 and 411 CE) takes the same theme of martyr-witness, drawn from etymology, and develops it further by focusing on the truth of the testimony's content. He begins with the verse from Psalm 115, which we just cited, and explains it by saying that the death of the martyrs is precious because of the blood of the Passion of Christ, who first suffered for them. He similarly cites another verse: "Everyone is a liar" (v. 11), which raises an objection: how were the martyrs witnesses to the truth if all men are liars? How can we simultaneously maintain the veracity of both the scriptures and the martyrs?

Augustine sees the solution to this difficulty in a passage from the Gospel reading he had just recited before his sermon: "When you are handed over, do not worry about how you will speak or what you will say; what you are to say will be given to you at that time. For it is not you who speak, but the Spirit of the Father speaking in you" (Mt 10:19–20).

If the martyrs spoke on their own, they would be liars, as all men are; but, by speaking through them, the Holy Spirit transforms them into truthful men, into truthful witnesses—into martyrs. One therefore becomes an authentic martyr [only] by the power and light of the Holy Spirit. Relying on his own power, a man can certainly be a witness, but he would be a witness only to the deceit that dwells within him, and not to the truth.

Augustine immediately applies this teaching to his own preaching: "If what we say to you came from ourselves, it would be the language of deceit. If, on the contrary, what we say to you comes from the Holy Spirit, it is the language of truth." Similarly, Christians should avoid speaking by themselves if they wish to speak the Truth and be true children of God. This is a general rule for Christian testimony in all its forms. In this way St. Augustine highlights an essential element of martyrdom: the divine truth to which [the martyr] bears witness.

What we have here is not a pessimistic denigration of humanity, but rather the expression of the bishop of Hippo's own awareness that the truth about which the martyrs testify, a truth that illumines the heart of man as well as the preacher himself: a truth that comes from God, is received by grace, and is not acquired by human effort. [Augustine] had already implied this claim at the beginning of the sermon by contrasting the disciples' fear, [which made them] abandon their master during the Passion, with the good thief's faith in Christ on the cross, where the action of grace appears in a special way: "Who taught (the thief) this faith, if not the one who hung next to him? The Lord was crucified beside him, yet He dwelt in his heart."

Sermon 326 presents an interrogation of martyrdom. The premise of the investigation is the imperial order to sacrifice to idols, implying Decius's edict of 250 CE obliging all Roman citizens to sacrifice to the gods on pain of death. The question of sacrifice brings to light the fundamental opposition between allegiance to the pagan gods and allegiance to the eternal God, as viewed through the lens of the evangelical directive to "sacrifice one's father and mother … for the name of Christ so as to obtain eternal life" (Mt 19:29). Also at issue is the question of [rival] authorities: that of the emperor threatening torture on the one hand, and on the other that of the eternal King which makes us scorn earthly authority in accepting the momentary derision of those who say, "where is your God?"

In Augustine's commentary on Psalm 118, when he treats verse 22, "Remove from me shame and contempt, for I have sought your testimonies," ["statutes" or "decrees" in modern translations; "testimonies" in the King James Version], Augustine changes the term *testimonia* to *martyria* and endeavors to show that this "testimony" (*martyria*) is in fact the prayer that Christ himself prays on behalf of his enemies, and likewise that which the martyrs, who are members of his body, offer on behalf of theirs. It is their testimony to the charity that feels compassion for the wretchedness of the persecutors when they mock the humility of the cross, the sole remedy for their pride. Now the martyrdom of Christ is honored by all; his shame and contempt are removed. Such is the case also for today's martyrs, who are now celebrated by the people (Sermon 9, n2–3).

II. THE MARTYRS' COMBAT

St. Augustine describes the combat waged by the martyrs under different aspects in different texts.

The Martyrs' Combat against Suffering

In Sermon 280, the first preached on the feast of Ss. Perpetua and Felicity, who died in Carthage in 203 CE, Augustine shows that the martyrs' merit comes from the way in which they scorn death and suffering.

The martyrs have overcome the instinctive enjoyment of life and fear of death that are so deeply engrained in our human nature. Despite its sorrow and its evanescence, all men love life and do everything possible to preserve it, or [at least] to delay its loss when they are ill. This is true for Christians, as well, though they hope for a better life. Our attraction to life is so keen that, were it possible, none of us would wish to die. Thanks to the strength of their love, hope, and faith, the martyrs have triumphed over this self-preservation instinct, together with the passions that it engenders and the fear of death that it nurtures. No bond keeps them bound to this life nor could retain them.

In this regard, Augustine makes allusion to the philosophical discussion on whether man's greatest fear is that of death or physical suffering, particularly through torture. He does not settle the debate, for one or the other fear could prevail over an individual and lead him to lie, or to speak a truth he wishes to hide; but as for the martyrs, they have overcome both the fear of suffering and that of death. Augustine is quick to add, however, that in the martyrs' case it is Christ who triumphs, for he lived in them. They have lived for him, not for themselves, and though dead, they have nevertheless eluded death: "He has triumphed in them who lives in them, so that those who have lived for him and not for themselves, though they be dead, may not die (*Vicit in eis qui vivit en eis ut qui non sibi, sed illi viverunt, nec mortui morerentur*)."

Augustine sees the manifest sign of Christ's action in the case of Perpetua, who, exposed to the blows of a rabid cow, nevertheless left the arena asking to the amazement of all around her "when shall we finally be led out to that cow, or whatever it was?" The text thus indicates her ecstatic state in the midst of torture. And so Augustine comments that it is Christ who pours into the martyr's soul spiritual delights that allow them to suffer only to the minimum extent necessary to test them, and never beyond their ability to resist.

In Sermon 330, from August 18, 397 CE, St. Augustine takes as the basis of his homily the text of St. Matthew: "If any want to become my followers, let them deny themselves and take up their cross and follow me. For those who want to save their life will lose it, and those who lose their life for my sake will find it" (Mt 16:25), together with the parallel from John (1 Jn 12:24–25).

On its face, the expression "to carry his cross" simply means to bear trials and tribulations and, following Christ, through hope, to the place where he has gone in Resurrection: namely to the Father. It is more difficult, however, to comprehend the prescription: "to deny himself." Augustine opposes the human thought that says, "how can one who loves himself deny or renounce himself?" with the word of God that says, "he who denies himself, loves himself." Indeed, by loving himself he loses himself, while in denying himself he finds himself. In martyrdom we see the two collide most clearly: the thought of man, his desire to live, his fear of dying; and the word of God inviting him to sacrifice his life. Here the thought reaches into the center of human life, to the love of self that is natural to all of us. How should we understand this paradox? This is not simply a literary or logical question; the whole meaning of martyrdom and Christian renunciation is at stake.

Augustine begins his explanation with the example of the planter put forth in John: when the planter sows his seed in the earth, he renounces it and it dies, and yet that is the price he must pay for the future harvest and for the delight that it brings. If he were to guard the seed in his granary, he would lose the harvest. Similarly, we are commanded to renounce ourselves in order to avoid losing ourselves through disordered love. Hence the renunciation of the martyrs is seen to be the necessary condition for the future harvests of the church.

Augustine fills out his explanation along the lines of his own thought regarding self-love. All people love themselves. Such love is natural and primary; there is no question of destroying it, since everything follows from this love that is created by God himself. This love can be ordered rightly, but it can also be disordered; the difference lies in the human heart's orientation to God.

So what is disordered love? It is the abandonment of God in order to love oneself. Yet is it not odd that in forsaking God, man is led to forsake himself and his interiority so that he may love and adhere to exterior things such as money? In this way the miser disrupts the balance [of love's order] when he places his soul on one side and money on the other, when God says to him that his soul is worth more than to gain the whole world (Mt 16:26). Whoever loves oneself to the exclusion of God loses oneself by holding on to external goods. Such a person cannot remain in himself, nor can he regard his own true worth. Hence the prodigal son, in leaving his father's house, lost his possessions and became destitute: "Yet for me, to adhere to God is my good, because if I do not live in him, I cannot remain in myself either, while he, remaining in himself, makes all things new."[3]

And what is rightly ordered love? It consists, for man, in the imitation of the prodigal son: to return to oneself, to recognize one's sin and unworthiness, and so to relinquish one's self, returning to God so as to love him above all else.

That is what the martyrs did, despising external goods, flatteries, threats, and fears. They returned to themselves and examined what they found there; they were displeased with themselves and [so] they raced to him who could give them form and life, in order to remain in him, putting to death in him that which they had begun to be in themselves—sinners—and preserving that which

3. See ibid., 1.V.II.XI.17.

he himself had created in their soul. That is what it means to "deny oneself," to "renounce oneself."

This interpretation proceeds directly from the experience of St. Augustine as he recounts it in the *Confessions* and as he expresses it in the two loves of the *City of God*: love of self to the point of contempt for God, and love of God to the point of contempt for self. Augustine sees a confirmation of this dynamic in the example of St. Peter, who, from an all-too-human perspective, wishes to keep Jesus from going to his Passion. In his fear for Jesus, Peter reveals his own fear of self-renunciation, and by loving himself [in this way] he denies Jesus. Yet after this triple denial, he weeps over his sin and then follows Jesus to the cross, so as to enter into life.

Sermon 331 takes up Matthew's injunction on renunciation: "Those who find their life will lose it, and those who lose their life for my sake will find it" (Mt 10:39). He offers two interpretations of this passage:

1. If you love your life, you lose it. So if you love it, then lose it: sow it here below so as to reap it in heaven, like a farmer who has to accept the loss of his grain at sowing time in order to obtain the harvest.

2. Do not love your life out of fear of losing it, like those who fear death and thereby appear to love their life. The martyrs would have certainly lost their life had they loved it in that way on earth and denied Christ in order to preserve it for a few years. On the contrary, they sought after Christ and confessed him, and in dying they held onto him. In losing their life, they gained immensely: they exchanged the life that scripture compares to straw for the crown of eternal life. "Is it not a good trade," Tertullian asks, "to give up a thing in order to receive an even greater one?"[4]

4. See Tertullian, *Ad martyras* V.6.

The Martyrs' Combat against the Temptations of the Devil and the World

Martyrdom is a combat against the temptations that come from either parents who want to save their children from death, from the world that tries to deter martyrs first by flattery and then by torture, or from the devil who is the master of this world and master of the art of temptation.

Augustine preached Sermon 284 on the feast of Ss. Marian and James, who were martyred at Lambesa in Numidia on May 6, 259 CE. Marian was a chanter and James a deacon. Their deaths are recounted by one of their lay companions. St. Augustine makes an allusion to their earthly relationships, especially to the joy of Marian's mother, who was called Mary. The aim of this sermon, the text of which is more extensive that the others, is to relate the passion of the martyrs to that of Christ, particularly with respect to the aspect of temptation.

The beginning of the sermon mentions a temptation that was frequent among the martyrs: their parents' efforts to make them recant. It makes allusion to the case of Perpetua, whose pagan father cunningly uses all the leverage of his familial relation to oppose the death of his daughter. Augustine sharply contrasts his despondency with Mary's jubilation: "When it was all over, the mother of Marian exulted, as joyful as the mother of the Maccabees once was. Now that the martyrdom was accomplished, she was tranquil about the fate of her son. She was happy not only for him, but also for herself, for having had such a child.... O Mary, so aptly named! O mother doubly blessed for having such a son and bearing such a name!"

Augustine frames the entire debate in terms of the battle within the human heart between two *delectationes*: the delights of the Lord and delights of the world, according to the categories typical of his anti-Pelagian period. We have, on one side, the attraction of the

Lord expressed in Psalm 26: "One thing I have asked of the Lord, one thing shall I seek; to dwell in the house of the Lord all the days of my life, to contemplate the delights of the Lord." On the other side we find the world's diabolical guile directed toward the martyrs, together with the subsequent torture to which the devil and the world must resort: "It was delectation opposed to delectation, it was delectation opposed to sorrow."

Note that in St. Augustine's Latin the term *delectation* designates the pleasure brought about by something good, whether sensible or spiritual. This term brings out the meaning of St. Augustine's reference to these two levels more than does the French [and English] term *pleasure*. St. Thomas will employ *delectatio* in this sense in the treatise on the passions where he will discuss this sentiment (*ST* I-II, qq. 30–34), distinguishing it more clearly from joy, which specifies a uniquely spiritual pleasure. Delectation designates the attraction that the good exerts upon the human heart. It can be good or bad, depending on whether it begets a good or bad love, ultimately either the love of God above all else or the love of self to the exclusion of God.

Attracted and inspired by the *delectatio Dei*—the divine delight—the martyrs wage their battle against all the attractions of the world. Augustine draws a comparison between this conflict and the temptations of Christ. He distinguishes between the two main occasions in which Jesus was tempted by the devil in his earthly life: the temptation in the desert, which was premised on flattery and disordered appetite, and the temptation of the Passion, which was premised on torture. *The temptation of the desert* is based on the seductions of the world, which are threefold: the bread being the figure of the concupiscence of the flesh; the promise of kingdoms being the representation of worldly ambition; and the temptation of curiosity being the illustration of the concupiscence of the eyes (see the three concupiscences of 1 Jn 2:16).

Christ allows himself to be tempted by the flatteries of the world in order to give us an example and to show us how to combat them by confronting them with the delectation that comes from God: to the promise of carnal sensuality, one must reply that God gives a greater joy, *delectabilior est Deus*; to the promise of superior honor and dignity, one must reply that the Kingdom of God is the most eminent of all; and finally, in the face of vain and foolish curiosities, one must hold up the truth of God, which alone does not deceive. In this way, following the martyrs' imitation of Christ, we can overcome the three seductions of the world: sensuality, curiosity, and pride.

At the end of his account of Jesus' temptation in the desert, St. Luke writes, "Having exhausted every temptation, Satan withdrew for a time," which is to say, St. Augustine remarks, until the day of the Passion when Christ was to undergo another form of temptation. *The temptation during the Passion* is one of trial, torture, violence, and persecution. It is carried out by the devil, who has entered into Judas to inspire his betrayal, and who will incite the Jews to single out Jesus for death. It is he who cries out through the mouth of the crowd, "Crucify him!"

In his Passion Christ has taught us, by his example, how to suffer: to insults and tortures, he responds with kindness and asks the Father to forgive them (Lk 23:34). He is like a sovereign doctor in the midst of frenzied madmen who take out their rage against him, and [yet] he will transform that rage into a remedy for their sin through the Holy Spirit whom he will send. It is by drinking with faith the blood of Christ shed for them that they will be healed and saved. After his Resurrection, he shows himself only to his disciples in order that he might not appear at any point to insult those who put him to death and in order to teach humility to his disciples. The power of the Spirit alone will subsequently transform them into preachers of the Gospel and into courageous witnesses. Hence Peter, who had proven so weak when he had relied on his own strength and his own willpower, experiences a complete change of heart when Christ directs his merciful gaze upon him.

Thus Marian and James, among others, who were all human beings like us, claimed victory over the double temptation of flattery and torment by struggling unto bloodshed. It is in this respect that we must imitate them.

At the beginning of Sermon 335, Augustine resumes this instruction. The conflict lies between the joy of the just and the joy of sinners: "While the just find their joy in the Lord, the unjust find their joy only in the ways of the world.... That is the first enemy to attack: we must first of all triumph over pleasure (*delectatione*) and only then over sorrow.... The world flatters us here below by promising us honors, riches and pleasures; the world frightens us by threatening us with sorrow, poverty and humiliation. If you do not despise its promises, how will you triumph over its threats?" In this combat, the martyrs have been victorious through the strength and love of Christ.

III. THE STRENGTH OF THE MARTYRS IS A GIFT FROM GOD

In Sermon 334, Augustine gives as a point of support for the battle waged by the martyrs the saying of St. Paul: "If God be with us, who will be against us?" (Rom 8:31). This inner support, as expressed in the phrase "the Lord is the upholder of my life" (Ps 53) is what allows them to hold onto the good even in the midst of torture and in the face of death. Yet such a bold claim requires proof, which St. Paul offers to us straightway: "God did not spare his only son, but delivered him up for us all." As St. Augustine remarks, "[the apostle] appeals to the Martyr of martyrs, to the Witness of witnesses, the Son of the Father who was not spared, but who was delivered up for us all.... Rejoice then that Jesus Christ has been given to us, and do not fear any of His enemies in this world." In Sermon 335, St. Augustine continues to build upon the same text of St. Paul's in which he hears the cry of the martyrs: "Who will separate us from the love of Christ? Will hardship, or distress, or persecution?" (Rom 8:35). He adds, "Without presuming any support of one's own, and loving Him who is glorified in his servants, so that he who is glorified is glorified in the Lord" (1 Cor 1:31). So it is the love of Christ that inspires and sustains the courage of the martyrs; he is the one at the center of their passion.

One particular theme [Augustine employs] to express this love is that of Christ the Bridegroom of the church, which appears prominently in his second Sermon for the feast of Perpetua and Felicity (281). The manly courage that they displayed, despite the weakness of their sex, has its source in this love: "They did well to attach themselves to this unique man, to whom the Church is presented as a unique and chaste virgin." He gave them the strength to overcome the devil, who once conquered all humanity through a woman. Augustine develops the theme according to the reversal brought about by Christ: women have now become strong because he became weak for them. "He who was shown to be invincible in them is the one who was made frail and weak for them. He filled them with strength so as to harvest them, he who was himself destroyed in order to fall to the earth like a fertile seed.... He, who for their sake mercifully allowed Himself to be born of a woman, has now allowed these women to die with courage and fidelity."

Another theme found throughout St. Augustine's preaching on the martyrs is the affirmation that their patience is a grace, something freely given by God and not earned through human effort.

Sermon 283, on the feast of the martyrs of Marseilles, is based on Psalm 61:6—"for my patience is from him"—in order to explain the patience of the martyrs and to insist on the importance of recognizing that [this patience] comes from God and not from oneself. Such is also the case with regard to the temperance that resists the attractions of sensuality. Indeed, he who does not know that God is the source of these benefits cannot thank him for them and may lose through his ingratitude even that which he has received. This is what sets the Spirit of God apart from the spirit of the world, for the Spirit of God is a spirit of charity, while the spirit of the world is one of pride. Better then, by far, is the one who gives thanks to God for the little he has received (and who shall subsequently receive much) than the one who prides himself on the extraordinary gifts he possesses, such as intelligence and memory, for example (which he will subsequently lose). Such is the grace with which we should oppose sensuality and sorrow: to hope in God and not fall back upon our own powers; and to confess the evils that are within us, relying upon God for the goods we need. The opposition is essentially one between humility and pride.

Only by relying upon God in this way have the martyrs been able to claim victory. On their own, they would not have been able to overcome their suffering; even if they had been, it would only have been a sign of brute toughness and not true patience. In any case, they could not overcome the devil. They needed God's help to obtain true faith and to suffer for it generously.

In Sermon 274 A, for the feast of St. Vincent, Augustine describes the many temptations one must overcome in order to truly confront pride. The devil seeks to seduce us with pleasures, and we must overcome him with temperance. He overwhelms us with pain and suffering, and we must triumph with patience. He wishes to make us fall into error, but we shall prove victorious through wisdom. His last resort is vanity, to which the devil appeals when he whispers to us, "what battles you have survived! Who could possible compare with you? What a glorious victory you have won!" The proper response of the Christian may be taken directly from Psalm 33:2: "My soul glories in the Lord, let the meek hear and be glad." The glory is in the Lord and in his grace, neither originating nor resting in me.

The proud, remaining trapped within themselves, cannot grasp this truth; it remains accessible only to the poor and the humble.

In Sermon 329, St. Augustine presents martyrdom as an exchange between Christ and his witnesses in which grace always takes the lead. He starts with a consideration of Psalm 115:5, "Precious in the sight of the Lord is the death of his holy ones," which he interprets to mean, "Their death is precious because of the death of the One who alone redeemed them all, He who was the grain of wheat multiplied through them." A great exchange was made on the cross: Christ opened the sack containing our ransom when his side was opened by the lance, allowing his own blood to flow for the sake of the whole world. It was then that the martyrs and all the faithful were redeemed. So when they themselves were put to the test, they rendered to him what he had given them; their blood thus bears witness to this original gift, [as St. John says]: "Just as Christ gave up his life for us, so we should also give up our lives for our brothers" (1 Jn 3:16).

Augustine further intensifies the sense of the martyrs' submission by taking up a saying from Proverbs (Prv 23:1) that he views in association with the Eucharist—"When you sit at a grand table, note well what is served to you, for you too must prepare as much"—a saying intended as an admonition to prudence for those who dine with the rich and powerful of the world. Interpreted in a spiritual sense, this grand table is that of Christ who gives himself as food and drink. Though the martyrs desire in turn to render this meal to Christ, they first come to realize that they have nothing to render that they have not already received from God. And so they ask themselves, "what can I render unto the Lord for all the good things he has rendered unto me?" Augustine insists on the term "render," which does not simply mean "give," but means that we have given our iniquity to him and he has given us his goodness. The psalmist [thus provides the appropriate response to this exchange when he] says, "I will take up the cup of salvation and call on the name of the Lord" (Ps 115:13), the cup of salvation meaning here the suffering of the martyrs who have agreed to follow Christ their physician, the One who first accepted the cup for their sake. The victory of the martyrs is therefore the work of Christ, who has conquered the world, in them.

A similar explanation may be found in Sermon 332, from the same era (410–12 CE): "You have come, poor as you are, in order to be filled. How does one prepare a suitable feast? Ask him who invited you to give you what you need to welcome him.... You have such little charity; do not attribute any merit to it.... Ask God to enlarge it, to make it perfect.... It is from Him that the martyrs have received the grace to suffer for him.... And it was He who also gave them the means to receive it."

One may also find the same idea in his commentary on Psalm 102 (verse 4).

IV. WHAT MAKES THE MARTYR IS THE CAUSE FOR WHICH HE SUFFERS

Another idea that regularly recurs throughout these sermons is the claim that the principal element defining Christian martyrdom is not the suffering that one undergoes but the cause for which one accepts it. "Above all else, you must remember this truth, which you must never forget and which should always be present in your mind: our suffering is not what makes us martyrs of God, but rather our justice" (Sermon 285). Many bear the burden of tribulations, and their suffering is common to all; yet the various causes of their suffering are quite different. Is there any kind of suffering that adulterers and malefactors do not endure, any pain from which thieves, murderers, and villains are exempt? Indeed, they also suffer what the martyrs suffer, but not for the same reason" (Sermon 337, no. 1). In the first homily on Psalm 68, he even says that "whatever torments the martyrs suffer, are they not the same as the torments of any robber, blasphemer or criminal?" (no. 9). And again in Sermon 325 he says, "do not be moved by the tortures and punishments of malefactors, blasphemers or any other enemy of peace and truth. It is not for the truth that they die; rather, they die in order to oppose themselves to the preaching of the truth, to the one who adheres to the truth, loves unity and charity, and who thereby reaches to eternity" (Sermon 325, no. 2).

Augustine loves to point out this difference by taking up the comparison of Christ on the cross with the two thieves who were crucified beside him: "The three were executed in the same location, the Lord placed in the midst of a pair of criminals. They placed the two robbers on his right and on his left, but the cause of these three executions could not have been more different. They were at the Lord's side, attached to the cross—yet what a distance separated them! They were crucified for their crimes, while he was crucified for ours. The thieves suffered justly, while Christ suffering willingly for our injustice."

[Augustine also points out] the great difference between the thieves themselves. The good thief displays the power not of his sufferings, but of pious confession (*pietas confitentis*): he obtained by his penitence what Peter lost through his fear; he believed in Jesus when the faith of the apostles was wavering. He merited a new cause for his suffering because he did not despise Jesus, even though they were condemned to the same torment.

Hence there are three crosses with three different causes. One thief insults Jesus, while the other confesses his crimes and commends himself to the Savior's mercy. The cross of Jesus was not so much an instrument of torture as a judgment seat, since from the height of the cross he condemns the one who insults him and delivers the one who believes in him (Sermon 285).

In Sermon 327, Augustine explains that the good thief was able to distinguish the cause [of his suffering], which was evil and rightfully merits punishment, from the cause of Jesus and the martyrs' suffering, which merits reward. Yet because of that awareness, Jesus promises him paradise on that very day when he merely asks to be remembered in his Kingdom.[5]

Sermon 275 indicates the proper cause [of suffering] by associating the terms freedom, truth, and justice: "Is it so difficult for our God, in order to confirm the predication of his name through the bodily deliverance of preachers into the hands of persecutors, to raise their souls to the heights of freedom, allowing them to bear witness to the truth while also being victims of iniquity? That is to say, if his faithful servants are to emerge victorious from this battle, it is justice rather than suffering that is most essential, for it is not what one suffers, but rather the motive for which one suffers that makes one a martyr."

V. MARTYRS ARE THE SEED OF THE CHURCH

Martyrs are the seed of the church, which produces its future harvest, according to a clear allusion to the words of Christ: "unless a grain of wheat falls into the earth and dies, it remains just a single grain; but if it dies, it bears much fruit" (1 Jn 12:24). "The earth

5. See *Sancti Augustini sermones post Maurinos reperti: Sermo Denis VI, 1–2*, in Miscellanea Agostiniana, testi e studi 1, edited by Germain Morin, 1:634 (Rome: Tipografia poliglotta Vaticana, 1930).

has been filled by the martyrs as with a seed of blood, and this seed has raised the harvest of the Church" (Sermon 286, no. 3). Even now this seed still produces its fruit: "They have affirmed Christ more by their death than by their life. And they affirm him today; they preach today. Their language is silent, yet their acts resound."

The deeds of the martyrs are their suffering, accepted for the sake of Christ. Therefore their death is precious, and fruitful, in the eyes of God. Augustine delights in pointing out this fact, particularly by contrasting the scorn of the people who oppressed the martyrs as they suffered with the people's veneration of the martyrs today. "Their death was precious in the eyes of God alone; and now it is precious in our eyes as well. It was then an opprobrium to be Christian, and the death of the saints was contemptible in the eyes of men. Indeed they were detested, loathed; it became a curse to say 'may you die by crucifixion and fire!' Yet today, which of the faithful does not covet such curses for themselves?" (Sermon 286, no. 3).

In his homily on Psalm 140, Augustine may even go so far as to compare the martyrs to manure, to the fertilizer of the earth, in connection with the verse "As one scatters the fat of the land upon the earth, so our bones have been scattered at the mouth of the grave." The Latin term *crassitudo*, which Augustine uses here, comes from *crassus*, meaning thick, fat, or crude. One could interpret it as referring to manure, which one spreads on the ground as fertilizer. "We know that the 'fat of the land' is made up of vile debris. That which is loathsome to men fertilizes the earth. One also reads in another psalm that the corpses of the holy ones are left upon the earth without anyone to bury them (Ps 78:3). But all those corpses became the fat of the land. Just as the land is fattened by loathsome and despicable debris, the earth is fertilized by that which the world has scorned, so that the harvest of the church may be multiplied in greater abundance.... [The death of the saints] is as loathsome to the world as it is precious to the Farmer. He knows how useful and bountiful it can be, for he knows what to look for and what to choose so as to bring about a fertile harvest; yet the world despises this death." Augustine applies this analogy even to Ss. Peter and Paul: "Peter and Paul were drawn from the manure, and when they were put to death they were despised; yet now their blood has nourished the earth and the harvest of the Church has emerged from it."

If the martyrs are the seed of the church, they are also its models, for we cannot be content merely to honor them; we should try above all to imitate them. Augustine forcefully reminds the faithful of this fact: "Remember that to honor [the martyrs] without imitating them amounts to nothing more than deceptive flattery. These solemnities have been established in the Church of Christ so that the community of Christ's members might be inspired to imitate the martyrs of Christ. That is the purpose of this feast and there is no other" (Sermon 325, no. 1).

Augustine then explains that the examples of the martyrs leave us with no excuse regarding our practice of the Gospel. One could say, "how can I imitate God, with whom man cannot enter into any comparison? How can I imitate Christ, who while clothed in mortal flesh was nevertheless truly God, the Word of God?" The martyrs have traced a sure path for us. In order to describe it, Augustine makes reference to Jesus' entry into Jerusalem: "Full of contempt for their bodies, they spread them out like clothing, as Jesus comes to conquer the nations, seated upon them as upon an ass" (see also Sermon 280, no. 6, with a slightly different illustration). We could still say that although Peter and Paul were men similar to us, we are nevertheless far from being their equals. [Yet] the objection collapses when we behold the martyrs: "illiterate men have received the crown, and have left us with no excuse for vanity. Are you going to say that you are not the equal of children, of young girls … or of faithful women such as St. Victoria?" (Sermon 325, no. 1).

Yet in striving to imitate them, we should at the same time remember that [their actions] were principally the work of grace: "In admiring the power which the saints wielded in their passion, we should proclaim the grace of the Lord. The martyrs did not want praise for themselves, but for the One of whom the Psalmist says 'my soul shall glory in the Lord.' Those who understand this truth are not proud or presumptuous; rather, they ask with trembling and receive with joy. They persevere, and preserve the grace they have received" (Sermon 285, no. 1).

In this way, the body of Christ is built up: "He has preceded us as our head, he waits for his members who must follow him; then the whole body will be complete, which is to say: Christ will be united to the Church. May we be counted among those who are written in the Book of Life, and may He grant us in this present life all that we need" (Sermon 286, no. 6).

9

MARTYRDOM IN THE THEOLOGY OF ST. THOMAS AQUINAS

With St. Thomas Aquinas, the spirituality of martyrdom unfolds within a theological synthesis nourished by scripture and the fathers, through which he interprets Christian experience and the tradition of the church.

The Beatitude of "those who suffer for the sake of righteousness" placed at the top of question 124 of the *Secunda secundae* is the first that Thomas devotes specifically to martyrdom, following immediately upon his treatment of the virtue of fortitude. In his commentary on Matthew, he claims that [this Beatitude] represents the perfection of the Beatitudes, certifying the Christian's adherence to them even in the face of tribulation. Thomas also builds upon St. Cyprian's *Letter to Martyrs and Confessors*, as well as the sermons of Maximus, the fourth-century bishop of Turin.

He draws even more from the work of St. Augustine and from the liturgical practices surrounding the cult of the martyrs.

St. Thomas structures his ethical thought around the virtues, differentiated as theological and moral, and perfected by the gifts of the Holy Spirit. Thus his first task will be to associate martyrdom with one of the principal virtues.

Insofar as martyrdom consists in a firm resistance to the attacks of persecution, it relates directly to the cardinal virtue of fortitude or courage, which provides us with the necessary strength of soul to adhere steadfastly to reason and truth even in the face of the gravest of difficulties (*ST* II-II, q. 124, a. 1–2). Yet [St. Thomas] will also show martyrdom's essential relation to faith in Christ and to the action of the Holy Spirit in charity. Martyrdom is not simply an act of human courage; it requires theological virtues as well. All the same, Thomas specifies that the martyr resists [difficulty] on behalf of truth and justice. What he is referring to here is the truth of faith in Christ and the justice of which the Sermon on the Mount speaks, conceived in contrast to the injustice of persecution and its cruelties.

The association of martyrdom with the virtue of fortitude is interesting because it allows St. Thomas to presuppose Aristotle's detailed analysis of the natural virtue of fortitude while integrating into it the Christian experience of spiritual combat as described by St. Cyprian in his litany on the African martyrs. He describes the martyrs as soldiers of Christ assembled in prison as in a camp, where they steadfastly resist seductions, threats, and tortures with an incorruptible faith. Aristotle, meanwhile, maintained that the supreme act of the virtue of fortitude was the valor of the warrior engaged in mortal combat. Thomas adopts this idea, but he transposes it to the Christian plane: the full realization of the virtue of fortitude consists for him in the valor of the martyrs, who have not only risked mortal danger, but have explicitly embraced death itself, a death that they endure as true soldiers of Christ. The martyr who wages spiritual combat on behalf of the faith therefore takes the place of the warrior and so becomes the model of Christian courage. Thus the liturgy may rightly chant, as it does for the mass of Ss. Fabian and Sebastian (on January 20), that "they were valiant in war."

However, the virtue of fortitude alone is not sufficient to give an adequate account of martyrdom. After all, as St. Thomas recalls, the Greek word "martyr" means "witness": the martyr is thus a witness to faith in Christ. As Maximus of Turin puts it, "The Catholic faith is the mother of martyrdom, that faith which the martyrs have sealed with their blood." In this way, faith and courage are linked together in the act of martyrdom: the truth taught by Christ is the cause of martyrdom, and also the primary focus and aim of the strength that the martyrs receive by God's grace. It is this faith that truly defines Christian martyrdom" (a. 2, ad. 1).

Martyrdom's connection to charity is equally essential, since charity is the motive cause of martyrdom. Martyrdom is a supreme act of courage inspired by charity, by the love of Christ, and so constitutes a demonstration of charity's perfection. The more one loves someone, the more one is prepared to suffer for his sake, whether that is by renouncing what is pleasurable or by enduring what is unpleasurable. The martyr is willing, for the sake of Christ, to renounce what man loves most of all, his own life, and to suffer torture and death, something that the animals themselves fear. He [thus] realizes the words of Christ according to St. John: "there is no greater love than to lay down one's life for one's friends" (Jn 15:13), and to the extent that it is animated by this love of Christ, martyrdom may be called the most perfect and meritorious act.

With the tradition of the church, Thomas believes that an act is not martyrdom in the proper sense of the term if the agent does not actually die on account of his faith in Christ (*ST* II-II, q. 124,

a. 4). He nevertheless accepts a certain extension of the concept of martyrdom based on the virtues that contribute to it. While maintaining that the truth of faith is the specific cause of martyrdom, he makes the distinction between faith in the heart and its external manifestation. This latter expression of faith does not consist in oral confession alone, but can include many other acts of virtue, so long as they are ordered to God. By means of this relation to God, all acts of virtue can become active expressions of faith and therefore be causes of martyrdom. Such was the case of John the Baptist, whom the church honors as a martyr because he suffered death for reproaching Herod and his adultery (*ST* II-II, q. 124, a. 5). Refusing to tell a lie on account of its prohibition by the law of God could also, in the same sense, serve as the cause of an authentic martyrdom (*ST* II-II, q. 124, a. 5, ad. 2).

The Holy Spirit likewise has its role to play in martyrdom. It intervenes first through charity, its first and principal gift, and then through the virtues that derive from it, producing what St. Paul calls "the fruits of the Spirit" (Gal 5:22), many of which apply especially to martyrs, such as patience, which is associated with fortitude (*ST* II-II, q. 136), and joy and peace, which are direct effects of charity (*ST* II-II, qq. 28–29). Yet we should not forget the gift of fortitude, which perfects the virtue of the same name (*ST* II-II, q. 139). According to St. Thomas, the Holy Spirit realizes in us a work that surpasses our natural capacities. We would like to finish the work we have undertaken and avoid the perils that threaten us, but who can do so with complete certainty? The Holy Spirit answers our expectations and fears by leading us to eternal life: the final culmination of our works and the deliverance from all our perils. In order to do so, the Spirit infuses into the heart and soul a confidence that drives out all fear, a confidence that manifests itself most especially in the martyrs, who have the greatest need for interior strength. One could also associate this confidence with the theological virtue of hope, which St. Thomas does not explicitly mention in the context of this question on martyrdom. Such hope is nonetheless the foundation of Christian fortitude and its direct confrontation with the fear of torment and death. This helps to explain why St. Thomas associates the gift of fear with the theological virtue of hope.

One can sense in this interpretation of fortitude a personal preoccupation of St. Thomas, particularly when he speaks of the human fear of not being able to complete the works one has undertaken. One might think that, having reached the middle of the voluminous second part of the *Summa Theologiae*, he asked himself whether he would ever come to finish it and consoled himself with the thought that it would find its final and most perfect completion in eternal life. And as it happened, the drafting of the *Summa* would be interrupted by Thomas's death in the middle of his treatise on the sacraments.

In conclusion, we should [briefly] mention the martyrs' reception of the gifts of the Holy Spirit associated with theological virtues: those attached to faith, such as knowledge and understanding (*ST* II-II, qq. 8–9), to hope, the basis of the gift of fear [of God] (*ST* II-II, q. 19), and to charity, which accompanies wisdom (*ST* II-II, q. 45). It seems fitting, in fact, that witnesses to Christ on the way to martyrdom would receive from the Spirit a more penetrating knowledge of the mystery that they confess, as well as a clearer and firmer understanding of what should be done and what should be avoided. Similarly, the Spirit would confer upon them a filial fear that would bind them to the heart of God and so expel all other fears contrary to their faith and hope. And last, in their reception of charity, they would also receive a new wisdom, the wisdom of the cross, which appears foolish in the eyes of men (1 Cor 1:18–25), but which alone can render martyrdom intelligible to us, allowing us to grasp its true meaning, function, and potency.

SELECTED BIBLIOGRAPHY

Aubé, Benjamin. *Histoire des persécutions de l'église jusqu'à la fin des Antonins.* Paris : Librairie Academique, 1875.

Allen, John L. Jr. *The Global War on Christians: Dispatches from the Front Lines of Anti-Christian Persecution.* New York: Image, 2013.

Aquinas, St Thomas. *Summa Theologiae.* Translated by the Fathers of the English Dominican Province. New York: Benziger Bros., 1947.

Avemarie, Friedrich, and Jan Eillem van Henten, eds. *Martyrdom and Noble Death: Selected Texts from Graeco-Roman, Jewish and Christian Antiquity.* New York: Routledge, 2002.

Bardy, Gustave. *La vie spirituelle d'après les pères des trois premiers siècles.* Paris : Bloud et Gray, 1935.

Beck, Brian E. "'Imitatio Christi' and the Lucan Passion Narrative." In *Suffering and Martyrdom in the New Testament*, edited by William Horbury and Brian McNeil, 28–47. New York: Cambridge University Press, 2009.

Bergman, Susan, ed. *Martyrs: Contemporary Writers on Modern Lives of Faith.* Maryknoll, N.Y.: Orbis, 1996.

Bouyer, Louis. *Histoire de la Spiritualité.* Vol. 1. Paris: Aubier, 1960.

Bowersock, G. W. *Martyrdom and Rome.* New York: Cambridge University Press, 1995.

Boyarin, Daniel. *Martyrdom and the Making of Christianity and Judaism.* Stanford, Calif.: Stanford University Press, 1999.

Budde, Michael L., and Karen Scott. *Witness of the Body: The Past, Present and Future of Christian Martyrdom*. Grand Rapids, Mich.: William B. Eerdmans, 2011.

Burrus, Virginia. *Saving Shame: Martyrs, Saints and Other Abject Subjects*. Philadelphia: University of Pennsylvania Press, 2007.

Castelli, Elizabeth A. *Martyrdom and Memory: Early Christian Culture Making*. New York: Columbia University Press, 2004.

Clark, Patrick M. "Servais Pinckaers's Retrieval of Martyrdom as the Culmination of the Christian Life." *Josephinum Journal of Theology* 17, no. 2 (Summer/Fall 2010): 250–76.

———. *Perfection in Death: The Christological Dimension of Courage in Aquinas*. Washington, D.C.: The Catholic University of America Press, 2015.

Collins, Adela Yarbro. "From Noble Death to Crucified Messiah." *New Testament Studies* 40 (1994): 481–503.

Cormack, Margaret, ed. *Sacrificing the Self*. New York: Oxford University Press, 2002.

Cunningham, Lawrence. "Saints and Martyrs: Some Contemporary Considerations." In *Theological Studies* 60, no. 3 (Sept. 1999): 529–38.

———. "Causa non Poena." In *More Than a Memory*. Dudley, Mass.: Peeters, 2005, 451–64.

De Cointet, P. "'Attache-toi au Christ': L'imitation du Christ dans la vie spirituelle selon S. Thomas d'Aquin." *Sources* 12 (1989): 64–74.

De Young, Rebecca Konyndyk. "Power Made Perfect in Weakness: Aquinas's Transformation of the Virtue of Courage." *Medieval Philosophy and Theology* 11, no. 2 (Fall 2003): 147–80.

Droge, Arthur J., and James D. Tabor. *A Noble Death: Suicide and Martyrdom among Christians and Jews in Antiquity*. San Francisco: HarperSanFrancisco, 1992.

Fields, Rona M. "The Psychology and Sociology of Martyrdom." In *Martyrdom: The Psychology, Theology and Politics of Self-Sacrifice*, edited by Rona M. Fields, Valérie Rosoux, Cóilín Owens, and Michael Berenbaum, 23–82 . Westport, Conn.: Praeger, 2004.

Fowl, Stephen E. "Believing Forms Seeing: Formation for Martyrdom in Philippians." In *Character and Scripture: Moral Formation, Community and Biblical Interpretation*, edited by William P. Brown, 317–30. Grand Rapids, Mich.: William B. Eerdmans, 2002.

Frend, William H. C. *Martyrdom and Persecution in the Early Church*. Malden, Mass: Blackwell, 1965.

Gregory, Brad S. *Salvation at Stake: Christian Martyrdom in Early Modern Europe*. Cambridge, Mass.: Harvard University Press, 1999.

Heyman, George. *The Power of Sacrifice: Roman and Christian Discourses in Conflict*. Washington, D.C.: The Catholic University of America Press, 2007.

Hovey, Craig. *To Share in the Body: A Theology of Martyrdom for Today's Church*. Grand Rapids, Mich.: Brazos Press, 2008.

Ignatius of Antioch. "Letter to the Trallians." In *The Apostolic Fathers*, 2nd ed. Edited by Michael W. Holmes, 99. Grand Rapids, Mich.: Baker, 1991.

Jensen, Michael P. *Martyrdom and Identity: The Self on Trial*. New York: T. and T. Clark, 2010.

Kinnard, Isabelle. "*Imitatio Christi* in Christian Martyrdom and Asceticism: A Critical Dialogue." In *Asceticism and Its Critics: Historical Accounts and Comparative Perspectives*, edited by Oliver Freiberger, 131–50. New York: Oxford University Press, 2006.

Matthews, Shelly. *Perfect Martyr: The Stoning of Stephen and the Construction of Christian Identity*. New York: Oxford University Press, 2010.

Middleton, Paul. *Radical Martyrdom and Cosmic Conflict in Early Christianity*. New York: T. and T. Clark, 2006.

———. *Martyrdom: A Guide for the Perplexed*. London: T. and T. Clark, 2011.

Mitchell, Jolyon P. *Martyrdom: A Very Short Introduction*. New York: Oxford University Press, 2013.

Moss, Candida R. *The Other Christs: Imitating Jesus in Ancient Christian Ideologies of Martyrdom*. New York: Oxford University Press, 2010.

———. *Ancient Christian Martyrdom: Diverse Practices, Theologies and Traditions*. New Haven, Conn.: Yale University Press, 2012.

———. *The Myth of Persecution*. New York: HarperOne, 2013.

Moreau, Jacques. *La persécution du christianisme dans l'Empire romain*. Paris: Presses universitaires de France, 1956.

Musurillo, Herbert, ed. *The Martyrdom of Perpetua and Felicity*. In *The Acts of the Christian Martyrs*, translated by Herbert Musurillo. New York: Oxford University Press, 1972.

Okure, Teresa, Jon Sobrino, and Felix Wilfred. *Rethinking Martyrdom. Concilium* 1 London: SCM Press, 2003.

Pelikan, Jarosłav. *The Preaching of St. Augustine: "Our Lord's Sermon on the Mount."* Philadelphia: Fortress Press, 1973.

Pinckaers, Servais, OP. *Sources de la moral chrétienne*. Fribourg: University Press Fribourg, 1985. Translated by Sr. Mary Thomas Noble as *The Sources of Christian Ethics*. Washington, D.C.: The Catholic University of America Press, 1995.

———. *La spiritualité du martyre… jusqu'au bout de l'amour*. Paris: Saint-Paul éditions religieuses, 2000.

———. *The Pinckaers Reader: Renewing Thomistic Moral Theology*. Edited by John Berkman and Craig Steven Titus. Washington, D.C.: The Catholic University of America Press, 2005.

———. "Reappropriating Aquinas' Account of the Passions." in Berkman and Titus, *The Pinckaers Reader*, 273–87. 2005.

Quasten, Johannes. *Patrology*. Vol. 2, *The Ante-Nicene Literature after Irenaeus*. Westminster, Md.: Christian Classics, 1984.

Radner, Ephraim. "Unmythical Martyrs." In *First Things: A Monthly Journal of Religion and Public Life*, no. 233 (May 2013): 53–55.

Rahner, Karl. "On Martyrdom." In *On the Theology of Death*. New York: Herder and Herder, 1964.

Royal, Robert. *Catholic Martyrs of the Twentieth Century*. New York: Crossroad, 2000.

Salisbury, Joyce E. *The Blood of Martyrs: Unintended Consequences of Ancient Violence*. New York: Routledge, 2004.

Seeley, David. *The Noble Death: Graeco-Roman Martyrology and Paul's Concept of Salvation*. Sheffield, UK: Sheffield Academic Press, 1990.

Slane, Craig. *Bonhoeffer as Martyr: Social Responsibility and Modern Christian Commitment*. Grand Rapids, Mich.: Brazos, 2004.

Smith, Warren J. "Martyrdom: Self-Denial or Self-Exaltation? Motives for Self-Sacrifice from Homer to Polycarp; A Theological Reflection." *Modern Theology* 22, no. 2 (April 2006) 169–96.

Sobrino, Jon. *Witnesses to the Kingdom: The Martyrs of El Salvador and the Crucified Peoples*. Maryknoll, N.Y.: Orbis, 2003.

Straw, Carol. "'A Very Special Death': Christian Martyrdom in Its Classical Context." In *Sacrificing the Self*, edited by Margaret Cormack. New York: Oxford University Press, 2002.

Streete, Gail P. C. *Redeemed Bodies: Women Martyrs in Early Christianity*. Louisville, Ky.: Westminster John Knox Press, 2009.

Tertullian. "Apology." Translated by Sydney Thelwall. In *Ante-Nicene Fathers*, Ch. 50, edited by Alexander Roberts, James Donaldson, and A. Cleveland Coxe, 3:55. Buffalo, N.Y.: Christian Literature Publishing, 1885.

———. *Epistle of the Gallican Churches Lugdunum and Vienna*. Translated by T. Herbert Bindley. New York: E. and J. B. Young, 1900.

Titus, Craig Steven. *Resilience and the Virtue of Fortitude: Aquinas in Dialogue with the Psychological Sciences*. Washington, D.C.: The Catholic University of America Press, 2006.

von Balthasar, Hans Urs. "Nine Propositions on Christian Ethics." In *Principles of Christian Morality*, by Joseph Ratzinger, Heinz Schürmann, and Hans Urs von Balthasar. San Francisco: Ignatius Press, 1986.

———. *Cordula oder der Ernstfall*. Trier: Johannes Verlag Einsiedeln, 1987.

Wicker, Brian. "Conflict and Martyrdom after 11 September 2001." *Theology* 106 (May–June 2003): 159–67.

———. "The Drama of Martyrdom: Christian and Muslim Approaches." In *Witnesses to Faith? Martyrdom in Christianity and Islam*, 105–16. Burlington, Vt.: Ashgate, 2006.

Wicker, Brian, Peter Bishop, and Maha Azzam. "Martyrdom and Murder: Aspects of Suicidal Terrorism." In *Witnesses to Faith? Martyrdom in Christianity and Islam*, 123–38. Burlington, Vt.: Ashgate, 2006.

Wilken, Robert Louis. "The Lives of the Saints and the Pursuit of Virtue." *First Things*, no. 8 (December 1990): 45–51.

Yearley, Lee H. "The Nature-Grace Question in the Context of Fortitude." *Thomist* 35 (Oct. 1971): 557–80.

York, Tripp. *The Purple Crown: The Politics of Martyrdom*. Scottdale, Penn.: Herald Press, 2007.

Young, Robin Darling. *In Procession before the World: Martyrdom as Public Liturgy in Early Christianity*. Milwaukee, Wisc.: Marquette University Press, 2001.

INDEX

The Spirituality of Martyrdom . . . to the Limits of Love was designed and typeset in Garamond Premier Pro by Kachergis Book Design of Pittsboro, North Carolina. It was printed on 60-pound Natures Book Natural and bound by Thomson-Shore of Dexter, Michigan.